PATTON

OPERATION COBRA AND BEYOND

Michael & Gladys Green

MBI Publishing Company

The authors would like to dedicate this book to their good friends Katie Baldwin and Dean and Nancy Kleffman for all their help and support during its completion.

First published in 1998 by MBI Publishing Company, 729 Prospect Avenue, PO Box 1, Osceola, WI 54020-0001 USA

The information in this book is true and complete to the best of our knowledge. All recommendations are made without any guarantee on the part of the author or Publisher, who also disclaim any liability incurred in connection with the use of this data or specific details.

We recognize that some words, model names and designations, for example, mentioned herein are the property of the trademark holder. We use them for identification purposes only. This is not an official publication.

MBI Publishing Company books are also available at discounts in bulk quantity for industrial or sales-promotional use. For details write to Special Sales Manager at Motorbooks International Wholesalers & Distributors, 729 Prospect Avenue, Osceola, WI 54020-0001 USA.

Library of Congress Cataloging-in-Publication Data
Green, Michael.
Patton: Operation Cobra and beyond/Michael & Gladys Green.
p. cm.
Includes index.
ISBN 0-7603-0498-X (pbk. : alk. paper)
1. Patton, George S. (George Smith), 1885-1945. 2. World War, 1939-1945—Regimental histories—United States. 3. United States. Army. Army, 3rd—History. 4. World War, 1939-1945—Campaigns—Western Front. 5. Patton, George S. (George Smith), 1885-1945. 6. Generals—United States—Biography. 7. United States. Army—Biography. I. Green, Gladys. II. Title.
D769.26 3d.G74 1998
940.54'21'092 98-23722
[B]—DC21 r98

On the front cover: In late July 1944, General Omar Bradley launched a plan called Operation Cobra in order to break through German defenses. The entire operation depended on an armored assault that would isolate the German divisions between Saint-Lo and the coast. Once accomplished, Bradley would rely on the flamboyant General George S. Patton to use his fast-moving armor to exploit the gap in the German lines. Pictured is a column of American M-4 Sherman tanks on a training exercise. *US Army*

On the back cover, top: To support Operation Cobra, First Army assembled one of the greatest concentrations of firepower in the European Theater of Operation . In conjunction with the massive air bombardment, American artillery played a critical role in the success of the initial breakthrough. More than 20 battalions of divisional and corps artillery were under the operational control of a single corps headquarters. Well-liked by the crew members, the dependable and robust M-1 howitzer seen here in full recoil was the workhorse of Patton's artillery support in Operation Cobra. *Real War Photos* ***Bottom:*** To overcome the supply problems that were hampering the Patton's Third Army, a temporary system known as the Red Ball Express was instituted. The Army's supply service devised a circular one-way truck route across France. It operated from the original invasion beaches to the fighting zone and back again. Between August 25 and September 5, the Red Ball Express brought 89,000 tons of supplies up to the Third Army. *National Archives*

Edited by: John Adams-Graf

Printed in the United States of America

CONTENTS

ACKNOWLEDGMENTS

Special thanks are due to the Patton Museum of Cavalry and Armor, the British Army Tank Museum, and The George S. Patton, Jr., Historical Society, whose support and help made this book possible. Thanks are also due to the U.S. Army Armor School Library at Fort Knox, Kentucky, and the Fourth and Fifth Armored Division Associations. George Hoffman, of the Sixth Armored Division Association, was kind enough to allow us to use pictures from his division's files. Individuals who made an extra effort in helping us out on this book include Charles Lemons (Patton Museum curator), Judy Stephenson (Armor School librarian), David Fletcher (British Army Tank Museum librarian), and Charles Province (president and founder of the Patton Historical Society). Other friends offering their kind assistance include Jacques Littlefield, Linda Brubaker, Dennis Riva, Ray Denkhaus, Kevin Hymel, Milton Hasley, Jr., Ron Hare, Dick Hunnicutt, Frank Schulz, Andreas Kirchhoff, Richard Byrd, Richard Cox, George Bradford, Mert Wreford, Richard Pemberton, and Karl and Carol Vonder Linden.

Note to the Reader

Due to space and format requirements, this book cannot be the definitive history of Patton's campaign in France during World War II. Instead, it presents a broad overview of that important period in Patton's life from about January through December 1944.

For those readers unfamiliar with Patton's career before and after 1944, a brief introduction and closing will help place the campaign in France in a historical perspective. Those who wish to learn more about Patton and his military campaigns will find a list of excellent books in the bibliography.

Another valuable source of information is the George S. Patton, Jr., Historical Society, which prints a semiannual newsletter devoted to the study of Patton. The society can be reached by writing to 3116 Thorn Street, San Diego, CA 92104-4618.

A visit to the world-famous Patton Museum of Cavalry and Armor, at Fort Knox, Kentucky, allows the viewing of various Patton artifacts as well as the weapons and equipment employed by both the Third Army and the Germans during World War II. Information on museum hours of operation and how to visit the museum can be obtained by writing to Building 4554, Fort Knox, KY 40121-0208.

INTRODUCTION

George Smith Patton, Jr., was born into an affluent California family on Wednesday, November 11, 1885. From a very early age, the young Patton expressed a strong interest in a military career. He received his appointment to the U.S. Army Military Academy at West Point in 1904. In 1909, the newly commissioned Patton began his military career as a Second Lieutenant in the Army's 15th Cavalry Regiment. By 1912, Patton was working for the Army's Chief of Staff.

Patton traveled to France in 1917 as part of the American Expeditionary Force (AEF) and a member of General John J. Pershing's staff. The ambitious young officer did not want to remain a staff officer. Convincing Pershing to transfer him into a combat outfit, Patton had the choice of commanding either an infantry unit or becoming involved with the Army's new Tank Corps. Never one to pass up a challenge, Patton selected the Tank Corps and never looked back. He came away from the war convinced that the tank offered great potential for future development.

After the war ended, Patton attempted to remain a tanker in spite of the Army's decision in 1920 to break up the Tank Corps and assign what remained to the infantry branch. When his attempt was unsuccessful, Patton decided to return to the cavalry, where he remained until July 27, 1940, when he returned to tank service. Patton received command of an armored brigade in the Second Armored Division, part of the Army's newly formed Armored Force that was established only days before on July 10, 1940.

The impetus for the formation of the Armored Force came from the German victories in Poland in 1939 and France in 1940. In the conquest of both countries, the Germans employed combined arms teams consisting of tanks, artillery, motorized infantry, engineers, and aircraft to overcome all resistance. This new method of waging war was referred to as *Blitzkrieg* (lightning war).

The Germans began their invasion of France on May 10, with their armored (panzer) divisions leading the way. The French Army, considered to be the best in Europe before the war, was outmaneuvered and outfought in a matter of a few weeks, officially surrendering to the Germans on June 25.

Of the 200,000 British troops sent to support France before the German invasion, 68,000 became casualties, along with most of their equipment. The great majority of remaining British troops fled the French coastal town of Dunkirk by ship or small boat between May 26 and June 3. Undeterred by their losses, British planners quickly began plotting a return to the continent. Only in that way would they be able to confront the Germans on the ground, liberate northwestern Europe, and put an end to the Nazi regime. The British received preciously needed help with their plans when the United States entered the conflict on December 19, 1941.

The Americans and British quickly agreed on making the defeat of Germany their number-one goal. Soon thereafter, British planners drafted a proposal, code-named "Roundup," for an amphibious assault across the English Channel into France. In 1942, the Americans and British were too weak to consider such a bold operation. Instead, they agreed to wear down the German military through military campaigns conducted around the shores of the Mediterranean. Part of the rationale for this decision was that such operations would provide the much-needed experience for preparing a cross-channel invasion of France.

The first large-scale operation undertaken by the inexperienced American Army was the invasion of French North Africa, code-named "Operation Torch," in November 1942. The invasion task force consisted of 900 ships and 86,000 American soldiers. The American generals who directed this operation found themselves destined to play important roles in the invasion of France 18 months later.

The overall commander of the American invasion forces involved in Operation Torch was Lieutenant General Dwight D. Eisenhower. Serving under Eisenhower was the recently promoted Major General George S. Patton, Jr., in command of the operation's ground elements of the Western Task Force. Previously, Eisenhower and Patton had served together as junior officers after World War I and were fairly good friends.

Patton's Western Task Force of 20,000 men and 250 tanks landed in French Morocco on November 8, 1942. Three days later, the Vichy (pro-German) French forces in French Morocco surrendered to the invasion forces. From mid-November 1942 to early 1943, Patton served as the military commander of French Morocco. The position was strictly political and not one that he enjoyed.

In March 1943, Eisenhower chose Patton to assume temporary command of the II Corps in Tunisia. Experienced German troops had mauled the II Corps at the Battle of Kasserine Pass in February, and Eisenhower felt that only Patton's aggressive zeal could restore morale and discipline.

On March 17, Patton took a revitalized II Corps into action against Italian forces in Tunisia. As his troops broke through the front lines, he saw a chance to cut the German supply lines. Much to his dismay, the local British commander denied his request to continue the offensive action. This would not be the last time Patton felt that higher commanders let an important opportunity slip away. In future operations, he often ignored orders from his superiors to pursue tactical opportunities when he saw fit.

The Germans quickly became aware of the threat posed by Patton's forces to their rear and attacked the II Corps on March 23. In contrast to the poor showing American soldiers had made at the Battle of Kasserine Pass a few weeks before when they faced a strong German counterattack, this time the II Corps, under Patton's helm, stood firm and threw back the German assault with heavy losses. One famous American general later wrote about the Americans' role in Africa, "On reflection, I came to the conclusion that it was fortunate . . . that the U.S. Army first met the enemy on the periphery, in Africa rather than on the beaches of France. In Africa we learned to crawl, then walk, then run. Had the learning process been launched in France it would surely have . . . resulted in an unthinkable disaster."

On April 14, Eisenhower arrived at II Corps headquarters in Tunisia and informed the victorious Patton that he would assume command of the newly formed Seventh Army, which would play an important role in the invasion of Sicily, code-named "Operation Husky." The amphibious assault on Sicily began on July 10, 1943. Within little more than a month, Sicily fell to the Allied Armies on August 17, 1943. The hard-charging Patton and the Seventh Army turned in a stellar performance during the campaign. Patton had no doubt that his success in the Sicilian campaign would lead to a top command position in the upcoming invasion of Italy or France. Much to Patton's dismay, two brief incidents during the Sicilian campaign almost cost him his military career.

Both incidents involved Patton's visits to local evacuation hospitals, where he viewed apparently unwounded soldiers who were suffering from battle fatigue (nervous breakdown). Patton did not understand how anyone could not control his fears. To the seemingly fearless general, any unwounded soldier unwilling to fight must be a coward. In both cases, Patton lost control of his temper and struck the helpless soldiers—a court-martial offense in the U.S. Army.

Word of the slapping incidents reached a shocked Eisenhower on August 16. Eisenhower issued Patton a very strong personal reprimand and forced Patton to apologize to all concerned. When word of the slapping incidents reached the American public, a public and Congressional outrage quickly arose that called for Patton's removal from any command position. Unwilling to court-martial one of his ablest commanders, Eisenhower saved Patton's career, knowing that he might need the outspoken general in the upcoming invasion of France. At the same time, Eisenhower decided that Patton did not have the balance and steadiness needed to command anything larger than a field army.

Instead, Eisenhower chose Major-General Omar N. Bradley to command the First Army and to lead the American forces during the upcoming invasion of France. Eisenhower knew that Bradley, unlike Patton, was calm and even-tempered and he had demonstrated his steady leadership skills in both North Africa and Sicily.

With American armies advancing in Italy and Bradley planning for his role in Operation Overlord, Patton remained in Sicily in a kind of limbo as commander of the ever-shrinking Seventh Army. Eisenhower was well aware that the Germans considered Patton one of the top American generals. Therefore, he sent Patton to different locations around the Mediterranean to confuse the Germans about where the next Allied invasion would commence.

In December 1943, Eisenhower received the appointment as Supreme Commander (over the heads of 366 senior generals) of all Allied forces involved in Operation Overlord. Once he arrived in London a month later, he quickly set about preparing his forces for the invasion of France.

Knowing of the difficult task ahead of him, Eisenhower decided that Patton could still make an important contribution to winning the war in Europe. Taking a chance, Eisenhower ordered Patton to report to England without telling him what he had planned for him.

Chapter One

PATTON AND OPERATION OVERLORD

Lieutenant General George S. Patton, Jr., arrived in England on January 26, 1944. Soon after, he visited the Supreme Headquarters, Allied Expeditionary Forces (SHAEF). General Eisenhower, the Supreme Commander of all Allied forces in Europe, told Patton he was giving him command of the Third Army when it arrived in England. Patton was elated. He also learned that General Omar Bradley, the commander of the First Army and his former subordinate, was now going to be his new boss, but Patton's happiness in rejoining the war effort no doubt tempered any resentment he may have felt about this role reversal.

Eisenhower's original plans for Operation Overlord had Patton's Third Army arriving at Normandy 10 days after Bradley's First Army's initial landing. Patton's job would be to seize the Brittany Peninsula with its many harbors and exploit the breakout of Bradley's First Army from the Normandy beachhead.

The assembly of Patton's troops, however, took longer than anticipated. The first 13 officers and 26 enlisted men of the Third Army headquarters staff arrived in England on January 28, followed by the remaining headquarters staff on March 21. At the time, armies were not shipped overseas as complete units. Rather, the elements, such as divisions, separate battalions, companies, group headquarters, corps headquarters, and army headquarters, arrived in England independently of each other, with divisions being the largest integral units to be shipped from the United States. Commanders assembled their armies and corps from these elements as they became available. Slowly,

As the aggressive and fearless commander of the first U.S. Army tank unit in World War I, Patton had earned a Distinguished Service Cross (DSC) and the temporary rank of colonel in 1920. When the U.S. Army shrank in size after the war, Patton reverted to his permanent rank of captain. It would take Patton another 18 years before he became a colonel once more in July 1938. *Patton Museum*

Pictured at the Desert Training Center in southern California, Major General Patton, Jr., takes a compass reading. Behind him is his personal M-3 light tank, sporting the pennant of the I Armored Corps. Patton acquired command of the Second Armored Brigade of the Second Armored Division on July 12, 1940, as a colonel. On October 1, 1940, Patton received his first star with a permanent promotion to the rank of brigadier general. He received his second star as a major general on April 4, 1941. On January 15, 1942, Patton took command of the I Armored Corps. *Real War Photos*

Below
Major General Patton commanded the Second Armored Division, at the Red River, Louisiana, maneuvers of 1941. In July 1942, Patton took charge of the II Armored Corps. This corps would be part of the American invasion of North Africa (code-named Operation Torch) in November 1942. The practice of having separate "type" corps disappeared in September 1942. *Real War Photos*

Patton's Third Army grew as the troop convoys from the United States reached England. By the end of May 1944, the Third Army consisted of four corps, the XV, VIII, XX, and the XII, which divided seven infantry divisions and six armored divisions among them. The total personnel strength of Patton's Third Army gradually rose to 250,000 men.

Patton, who believed that troops' morale improved when they saw their commanding officers, made it a point to visit as many of his new units as possible. During his many visits to Third Army units in England, the always immaculately uniformed Patton tended to give very similar, profane pep talks to his men, because he felt this was the level on which the common enlisted man spoke. Patton once stated, "You can't run an army without profanity." One of his inspirational addresses began, "I want you men to remember that no bastard ever won a war by dying for his country. He won it by making sure the other dumb bastard died for his country. All this stuff you've heard about America not wanting to fight, wanting to stay out of this war, is a lot of horseshit." He normally ended his pep talks with "I'm not supposed to be commanding this Army. I'm not even supposed to be in England. Let the first bastards to find out be the God-damn Germans. I want them to look up and howl, 'Ach! It's the God-damn Third Army and that son of

a bitch Patton again!' All right, you sons of bitches, you know how I feel. I'll be proud to lead you wonderful guys into battle anywhere, anytime. That is all!"

Prior to the planned invasion of France, England became a vast ordnance depot of American equipment. Here, at an undisclosed location in England, is a vast collection of American tracked and wheeled vehicles. The vehicles in the foreground are M-4 Sherman medium tanks. It took 50 hours to prepare a Sherman tank before it could be issued to a combat unit. When a vehicle left an ordnance depot, it was completely supplied, including ammunition and rations. *National Archives*

Patton salutes his troops in England in early 1944. Patton always believed that officers should lead by example, and as a result was always on parade, dressing to perfection as an example for everybody in the Third Army. He once explained to a fellow general that "I want the men of Third Army to know where I am, and that I risk the same dangers that they do. A little fancy dress is added to help maintain the leadership and fighting spirit that I desire in the Third Army." *Real War Photos*

Patton always tried to emphasize in speeches to his men that armies succeeded in battle due to teamwork. He often stated, "An army is a team. It lives, eats, sleeps and fights as a team. This individuality stuff is a bunch of bullshit. The bastards who write it for the Saturday Evening Post don't know any more about real battle than they do about fucking." *Real War Photos*

Most Third Army soldiers heartily enjoyed Patton's somewhat vulgar speeches. Because Patton's boisterous reputation preceded him, Eisenhower made a point of telling him that he was not to make any public speeches without the commander's express permission. He ordered Patton to guard all his statements so there would be no chance of misinterpretation. Eisenhower had been forced on earlier occasions in French Morocco and in Tunisia to smooth over problems caused by Patton's inability to keep his opinions to himself. The Supreme Commander obviously did not want to see Patton commit any verbal blunders that might attract the attention of the American public, Congress, or the press.

Patton apparently decided to ignore Eisenhower's order, however. On April 25, 1944, while in England, General Patton made a public speech to a British women's club. Though Patton believed that his remarks would be off the record, portions of his speech leaked to the press and caused a furor in the United States and overseas. It was at this point that both Eisenhower and General George C. Marshall, the Chief of Staff of the Army and the chairman of the Joint Chiefs of Staff Committee, were ready to fire Patton, stripping him of his combat command.

At the last moment, Eisenhower had second thoughts about sacking one of his most aggres-

A very pleased Eisenhower attaches the third star of a lieutenant general to the jacket of a beaming Patton. Patton achieved the rank in March 1943 while in North Africa. The previous month, Eisenhower had received his promotion to the rank of general (four stars). Patton would write: "Of course, I was originally selected for 'Torch' through the direct action of Ike (Eisenhower) and therefore I owe him a great deal. On the other hand, I have paid my way ever since." *Patton Museum*

Pictured together are Dwight D. Eisenhower and George C. Marshall, both four-star generals at the time. Eisenhower graduated from West Point in 1915. During World War I he served in various positions as an instructor in the United States
Army, and after the war he served in various tank units until 1922. It was during this period that Eisenhower met Patton,
who had commanded tanks in combat. They both had a strong belief in the future of tanks, and struck up a somewhat
troubled relationship that lasted until Patton's death in December 1945. Marshall graduated from the Virginia Military
Institute in 1910. In World War I, he served as a staff officer in France. As one of the Army's best and brightest young officers, he rose quickly in rank. By September 1939, Marshall had become the Chief of Staff of the Army, the most senior
army command position. It was Marshall who handpicked Eisenhower for the job of Supreme Commander. *Real War Photos*

sive generals. Instead, he made a crucial decision to keep Patton in command of the Third Army. In a letter to Marshall, Eisenhower explained why he decided to retain Patton, stating, "The relief of Patton would lose to us his experience as commander of an army in battle and his demonstrated ability of getting the utmost out of soldiers in offensive operations." Eisenhower also wrote to Patton informing him that his job was safe "solely because of my faith in you as a battle leader and for no other motive."

The German Army in France

On the eve of the Allied invasion of France, the Germans had 59 combat divisions in France, most of which were static and only suitable for limited defense employment. Due to a shortage of transport vehicles (both wheeled and tracked), these static divisions depended on horses to move their heavy equipment. The other nonstatic divisions were considered fit for both offensive and defensive operations due to their relative mobility and higher-quality personnel. They included 13 army infantry divisions, 2 Luftwaffe parachute divisions, 10 panzer (armored) divisions, and 1 panzer grenadier (mechanized infantry) division. There were also 3 independent panzer battalions equipped with Tiger tanks.

Eisenhower fires a .30-caliber machine gun from the hip at a training base in England. Despite their long friendship, Patton often made disdainful remarks about Eisenhower's lack of combat experience to his staff and in his diary. This was an unfair observation about Eisenhower, who had tried mightily to see action in World War I. After the slapping incidents in Sicily, the friendship between the two men began to cool. Eventually, Patton's relationship with Eisenhower was conducted at a strictly professional level. *Real War Photos*

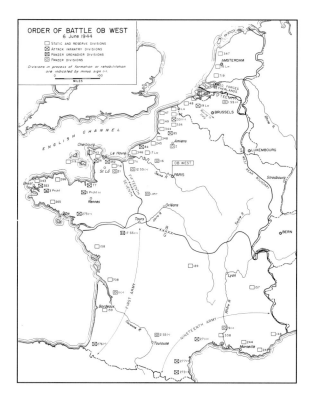

By late 1943, the Germans became convinced that the Allies would launch a major invasion of the European Continent sometime in 1944. Between November 1943 and June 1944, the number of combat divisions in the West increased from 46 to 58. The divisions were divided among four armies: the 1st, the 7th, the 15th, and the 19th. Overall commander of the four German armies lay with *Oberbefehlshaber West* (OB WEST) with headquarters in Paris. This map shows the deployment of the German ground forces on the day of the Allied invasion. *U.S. Army map*

Hitler made 69-year-old Field Marshal Gerd Von Rundstedt, shown here, Commander in Chief West in March 1942. Rundstedt was a Prussian aristocrat who joined the German Army in 1892. When the Allies invaded France in June 1944, Rundstedt had four German armies under his command with a total of 58 divisions. Unhappy with the conduct of the campaign in France, Hitler relieved Rundstedt of his command in early July 1944. *Real War Photos*

On paper, all of the German panzer divisions, plus the single panzer grenadier division in France, fell under the command of a headquarters unit referred to as Panzer Group West, officially activated in January 1944. In March 1944, Generalfeldmarschall (field marshal) Erwin Rommel, commander of Army Group B, managed to get three of the panzer divisions transferred to his army group. The remaining panzer divisions in France could not be moved without Hitler's permission. In July 1944, Panzer Group West was upgraded and designated as the Fifth Panzer Army.

The majority of German divisions in France at the time of the Allied invasion fell under the command of one of four armies: the First (holding the Atlantic coast of France), the Seventh (occupying Brittany and most of Normandy), the Fifteenth (defending the Pas de Calais area all the way up to the Dutch port of Antwerp), and the Nineteenth (defending the French Mediterranean coast). All four armies fell under the overall control of Generalfeldmarschall Gerd von Rundstedt, whose headquarters were in Paris.

Of these four German armies, the Fifteenth was the largest and best equipped. It consisted of four corps that controlled 14 army divisions and three less-reliable Luftwaffe field divisions.

Serving under Rundstedt was Field Marshal Erwin Rommel, shown here greeting Hitler. Rommel received the appointment to command Army Group B in November 1943. This army group contained 29 divisions, and bore direct responsibility for the defense of the Normandy area of France. Rommel gained fame fighting the British, and later the Americans, in North Africa between 1941 and 1943. It was in North Africa that he gained the nickname the "Desert Fox." In July 1944, Rommel was severely wounded during an air attack and forced to give up command of Army Group B. *National Archives*

In addition, the Germans had built more extensive coastal defense fortifications in the Fifteenth Army sector than in any other area, including the Seventh Army sector, where the Allied invasion eventually took place. The Seventh Army had 14 divisions, including a static division divided into four corps. Overseeing the four German armies were two Army Groups: Army Group G, which controlled the First and the Nineteenth Armies; and Army Group B, which controlled the Seventh and the Fifteenth Armies.

The large concentration of resources in the Fifteenth Army sector reflected the German conviction that the Allies would strike in that area, as it occupied the closest point to England. An Allied landing here would guarantee the most direct route to Germany and its industrial heart, the Ruhr. Strategic Allied success in this sector could cut off the whole of the German forces to the south.

In the summer of 1943, Hitler ordered construction of V-1 rocket launching sites in the Calais area and in Belgium. Convinced of the overwhelming threat the V-1 rockets posed to the Allies, Hitler thought they would change whatever previous invasion plans the Allies had and force them to invade Calais. Patton's phantom First Army Group only heightened Hitler's beliefs.

For the German military, June 1944 was not a good month. The Allies landed successfully in Normandy on June 6, and the Soviet Army launched a major summer offensive on June 22. By the end of June, before the offensive ran out of steam, the Soviet Army managed to tear a 250-mile hole in the German lines (destroying 25 divisions in the process) and entered eastern Poland. Pictured is a small column of Soviet Army ISU-122 self-propelled guns on a break somewhere in Poland. *Patton Museum*

Sitting together are Patton and Lieutenant General Omar Bradley. In March 1943 Bradley became the deputy commanding general of II Corps (in North Africa) under Patton. During the battle for Sicily in July and August 1943 Bradley led the II Corps under Patton's Seventh Army command. Bradley received a promotion, over the more senior Patton, as commander of the First Army in late 1943. *Patton Museum*

Operation Fortitude and Operation Overlord

Prior to the invasion of France, the Allies came up with a deception plan to mislead the Germans, called "Operation Fortitude." The goal of Operation Fortitude was to mislead the Germans into believing that the Pas de Calais area of France, rather than Normandy, would be the main invasion site. Operation Fortitude also sought to convince the Germans that any other landings in France would be merely a diversion to draw their attention away from Pas de Calais, a mere 20 miles away from the English coast. Eisenhower's staff created a mythical First Army Group, with up to 30 divisions in its organization. This phantom force supposedly

had its location near Dover, just across the Channel from Calais. To fool the occasional German reconnaissance plane, Allied planners used construction crews to build dummy military bases and dotted them with inflatable tanks and vehicles. They also anchored a large number of inflatable rubber landing craft in the Thames River estuary.

The Allies already knew from breaking Japanese diplomatic and military codes before the war that the Germans did not consider the Normandy area a viable landing site for a major invasion. The Americans referred to all the information gathered from reading the Japanese codes as "Magic," and shared it with the British. Japanese diplomats and military

American assault troops cross the English Channel toward France, aboard a Coast Guard-manned vessel. Shortly before midnight on June 5, 1944, elements of a British and two American airborne divisions took off from various airfields in southern England. Their job was to secure exits from various Normandy beaches, in preparation for the main Allied landing on the next morning. The main invasion force consisted of elements of three American, two British, and one Canadian division. These troops set sail in 5,000 vessels of all different shapes and sizes. *U.S. Coast Guard*

attachés sent detailed reports on every aspect of the German war effort and plans back to Japan throughout the war. This information, in conjunction with the British breaking of German military codes, referred to by the British as "Ultra" and shared with the Americans, provided Allied senior military leaders with advance warning of many German short- and long-term plans. The Germans and the Japanese had complete faith in their "coded" radio communication system. They never suspected the Allies compromised it at any point during the war.

Well aware of the high regard the Germans had for Patton's command skills, Eisenhower correctly assumed that the Germans believed Patton would lead any invasion of France.

Eisenhower therefore made Patton commander of the phantom 1st Army Group, and saw to it that known enemy agents received information on the status of Patton's forces.

To heighten the German perception that Patton's 1st Army Group would invade the Pas de Calais area, Allied naval units conducted extensive maneuvers in the English Channel near the location of the phony army. To simulate a large military force, dummy radio traffic was transmitted from the area. In the weeks before the actual Normandy invasion, Allied airmen dropped more bombs on Calais than anywhere else in France.

The real Allied invasion force of 5,000 ships with 130,000 Allied soldiers stood off the Normandy coast as dawn broke on June 6, 1944.

To defend the Normandy beaches from possible Allied landings, the Germans had built a series of coastal fortifications known as the Atlantic Wall. The basic component of the Atlantic Wall consisted of strong points dotting the French coastline. Pictured is a German pillbox, armed with an antitank gun, that fell to American soldiers on the first day of the invasion. *National Archives*

The Allies' main strategy, in Eisenhower's words, was to "land amphibious and airborne forces on the Normandy coast between Le Havre and the Cotentin Peninsula and, with the successful establishment of a beachhead with adequate ports, to drive along the lines of the Loire and the Seine Rivers into the heart of France, destroying the German strength and freeing France."

The seaborne assault was under the overall command of British General Bernard Montgomery, who also commanded the 21st Army Group. This command became the controlling headquarters for the two Allied armies scheduled to make the invasion. The British Second Army under Lieutenant General Sir Miles C. Dempsey was to assault on the left; the First Army under Bradley (promoted now to lieutenant general) on the right.

The Operation Overlord invasion began on a broad front against 50 miles of French coastline. Aerial bombardment of beach defenses began after midnight, with the naval bombardment starting shortly after sunrise. At 6:30 A.M. the first waves of assault infantry and tanks landed on the invasion beaches. German defenses consisted of underwater obstacles, mines, and barbed wire. Concrete pillboxes and gun emplacements would deliver direct fire on the beaches. All exits leading inland had antitank walls and ditches, minefields, and additional barbed wire. Farther inland, mortars and artillery could deliver indirect fire. Thousands of heavy wooden stakes dug into the ground hindered glider landing attempts.

Naval gunfire and air bombardment hammered German artillery and mortar positions, pillboxes, and gun emplacements. German ground elements put up stubborn resistance, and bitter fighting developed in some areas. On Omaha Beach more than 2,500 Americans became casualties. In addition, the two American airborne divisions suffered losses of at least 2,500 men. Despite these losses on the first day

U.S. Army Organization in World War II

In both the Allied and German military organizations, divisions were armies' basic operational units. They were the smallest composite units able to operate completely independently with their own hospitals and motor pools, and they ranged from a personnel strength of 10,000 to 20,000. As the war progressed, the structure and organization of divisions in both the Allied and German military underwent a number of changes in response to many different factors, including experience gained in combat.

The American Army maintained 89 combat divisions in World War II with an average strength of 13,400 men each. In turn, each American combat division received support from 30,000 men in nondivisional units, of which 16,500 were designed for close support in the combat zone and 13,500 for rear-area employment. The American Army ground troops numbered about four million men at their peak in World War II. Of this total, roughly 30 percent were in divisions, 40 percent in nondivisional unit types intended for the combat zone, and 30 percent in nondivisional unit types intended for rear-area employment.

Divisions came under the operational control of the corps. The corps was a highly flexible force made up of divisions, but lacked a fixed organization. The job of the corps commander and his staff officers was to give direction to divisions in combat. One American general described the corps commander as, "the last man toward the rear who directs tactical fire on the enemy. He is the commander who conducts the battle."

The corps also controlled pools of nondivisional combat units, such as corps artillery, engineer, tank, and tank destroyer, which were handed out to divisions based on needs and availability. By 1942, it was general Army policy in organizing its divisions to permanently assign only such forces as were needed for normal operations (in military terms, referred to as "organic"). Armored divisions had more organic support units than infantry divisions due to the belief that they would operate farther away from the mass of forces.

While American Army divisions were fairly standardized, corps varied a great deal in size and strength. One corps commander described it as an amorphous, elastic tactical unit that "expands and contracts according to the allocation of troops from higher headquarters based on the enemy, the terrain, and the contemplated missions." A corps could have anywhere between 100,000 to 300,000 men depending on the number of divisions assigned to it.

By 1945 the American Army had 24 corps, of which only one remained in the United States throughout the war. Twenty-two corps were actively engaged in combat operations at some time during World War II. There were 34 Army generals that commanded corps in battle.

The unit above the corps was the field army. Like the corps, the army consisted of a number of combat and combat-support units. While the corps, which was smaller than the field army, was a tactical grouping of divisions and supporting units, the field army was a tactical and administrative organization. The only part of an army that remained permanent was the headquarters staff and some signal units. Headquarters staff provided the core and framework of the army. The signal units transmitted the orders and directions of the headquarters staff to subordinate units. The Third Army headquarters consisted of the regulation 450 officers and 1,000 enlisted men at full strength. Other army headquarters staff in Europe grew much larger than regulations technically allowed.

The 1,450 men of the Third Army headquarters staff were divided into two groups. The first consisted of five general staff sections led by colonels and the second of 18 special staff sections led by colonels or lieutenant colonels. The job of the special staff sections involved controlling the many attached units that made up the Third Army. Examples of units attached to armies included artillery, engineer, quartermaster, and tank-destroyer formations.

The number of men that made up an army depended on how many divisions were assigned to it when organized. Divisions did not always remain part of the same army. All divisions, except those in army reserve, were intended to be passed on to various corps, shifting from one corps to another at the discretion of the army commander.

The next command level above the Army is the army group. It is the largest field organization under a single commander, and it may consist of as many as a million men. The army group headquarters exists primarily to provide tactical control and coordination for its subordinate elements. The army group commander controls the operations of the armies placed under his command. During World War II, three U.S. Army Groups saw employment in order to control the eight different field armies in France and Germany.

Corps, like divisions, were shifted by army group commanders from one army to another at their discretion. Between August 1944 and the German surrender in May 1945, a total of six corps served under Patton's Third Army. They included the XII, XX, VIII, III, XV, and V Corps. Divided among these six corps were 42 divisions that spent time as part of Patton's Third Army. Of those 42 divisions, 26 were infantry, 14 were armored divisions, and 2 were airborne.

In the wartime American Army, major generals (two stars) normally commanded divisions. Lieutenant generals (three stars) tended to command corps and full generals (four stars) commanded army groups. There were exceptions to these general rules. Brigadier General (one star) Milton B. Halsey commanded the 97th Infantry Division of the Third Army from January 1943 till the end of the war before being promoted to Major General.

Before the first Allied assault troops reached the beaches of Normandy, Allied planes concentrated on trying to smash the German beach defenses. The Allies also employed naval fire support in this role. The first targets of the air bombardment were the German coastal batteries, capable of interfering with the invasion fleet. Second were the coastal defensive positions, equipped with infantry weapons designed to stop assault troops from advancing off a beach. Pictured are Martin B-26C medium bombers, after a bomb run on German coastal defenses. *Real War Photos*

The assault troops from Bradley's First Army landed on two beaches code-named Omaha and Utah. Of the two American landings, the battle for Omaha beach proved the tougher of the two. Allied intelligence personnel had failed to pick up the deployment of additional German troops in the area. Total casualties on Omaha beach on June 6, totaled almost 3,000 men killed, wounded, and missing. On Utah beach, the Americans lost only 197 men, including 60 lost at sea. Pictured is an American soldier who never made it off the beach. *National Archives*

of the invasion, Allied commanders considered the casualties to be low. They had prepared their staffs to handle at least 12,000 killed or wounded in the First Army alone.

By nightfall on D-day, five American divisions, the 1st, 4th, and 29th Infantry Divisions, and the 82nd and 101st Airborne Divisions established themselves in Normandy. Also ashore were advance detachments of the headquarters of Major General Leonard T. Gerow's V Corps and Major General J. Lawton Collins' VII Corps.

First Army Roadblock

By the end of the first week, the Allied beachhead in France was fairly secure. The German coastal defense system had fallen apart. This accomplishment did not come without a high cost. In the first 10 days of fighting the Germans, the First Army lost 3,282 dead, 12,600 wounded, and 7,959 missing.

The VII Corps of the First Army quickly began moving in a northwesterly direction to seize the port of Cherbourg, at the tip of the Cotentin Peninsula. The capture of Cherbourg was very important to the Allies if they hoped to get a major port into full operation before the end of the summer. Without a major port, the Allies feared that bad weather would prevent supplies from being unloaded across the open invasion beaches.

The Army's 90-mm antiaircraft gun M-1, shown here, could reach targets up to 40,000 feet. In the wartime American Army, nondivisional antiaircraft units were found at corps level. In the early days of World War II, senior army leaders believed that antiaircraft units needed to be concentrated in corps' rear areas. They did not believe that forward units would be subjected to heavy air attacks. Combat experience in North Africa showed them the error of their ways. In 1944, antiaircraft units were located directly behind the American Army's front lines, where they could be the most useful. *National Archives*

The VII Corps, with three divisions, forced the surrender of Cherbourg on June 27, after fierce fighting. The drive up the Cotentin Peninsula cost the VII Corps 22,000 casualties, while the Germans lost 39,000 prisoners and an unknown number of dead and wounded. The seizure of Cherbourg with its port facilities proved a hollow victory. German engineers had so thoroughly demolished the port that it took months before full operations resumed.

The Allied military leaders had planned to control the whole of Normandy and Brittany by July 6. Having gained this area, the Allies would have had access to more than 500 miles of French coastline and many port facilities. The Allies could then bring in all the men and material needed to build up their forces. In addition, the area envisioned under Allied control (known as a *lodgment* in military terms) would have allowed maneuver room for ground troops and suitable terrain for at least 27 airfields. The Allies had hoped to have 62 fighter squadrons in operation on these 27 airfields.

By early July, almost a million Allied troops, 500,000 tons of supplies, and 150,000 vehicles had landed in France. First Army had 13 divisions, including two armored and two airborne, divided into four corps, the V, VII, VIII, and the XIX. The VIII Corps headquarters actually belonged to Patton's Third Army. It was temporarily attached to the First Army until the Third Army became activated on August 1, 1944.

The most numerous divisional artillery piece in the American Army in World War II was the 105-mm howitzer M-2. It first entered service in 1928 in small quantities, classified as a light artillery piece. It was not until 1941 that production output of the weapon was increased. A total of 8,536 units were built during the war years. With a full crew of eight, the howitzer could fire up to eight 33-pound rounds per minute, to a top range of 12,500 yards. Each wartime infantry division had three battalions of 12 105-mm howitzers. *National Archives*

These four corps held a front some 50 to 55 miles long. Despite these impressive figures, the Allies still found themselves confined to a very small part of France. In some areas, the Allied lines extended less than four miles into France, an area less than one-fifth the size they had planned on controlling by early July.

An army communication truck packed full of radio equipment, shown here, was critical to the Signal Corps, an important part of every army, corps, and divisional headquarters unit. Members of the Signal Corps had the job of operating and maintaining all the communications equipment for the various military organizations. To pass messages between various levels of the Army, the Signal Corps had various tools. These tools included teletypes, telegraphs, telephones, and radios. Radios saw their first widespread use during the fighting in North Africa. *National Archives*

The Allies also failed to acquire the French port facilities they so badly needed. Most of the Allied troops and material still had to come across the original landing beaches. There was a real fear among some Allied leaders that the opposing 650,000 Germans troops could still destroy the Allied beachheads.

Fortunately, the Allied ground forces in France were well within range of both air and naval support based in England. It was this air and naval support that did much to keep German forces from overrunning the beachhead. Allied air power paralyzed all German Army movement during the daylight hours and even made movement at night difficult. The long-range and accurate fire of Allied battleships also proved a deadly surprise to the German forces.

At the same time when the VII Corps headed northwesterly up the Cotentin Peninsula to capture the port of Cherbourg, other elements of the First Army center sector slowly headed southward. There was little progress for a number of reasons, including Bradley's desire to commit most of his resources to the VII Corps' drive and the numerous terrain obstacles that slowed his forces.

The left flank of the First Army occupied broken and uneven terrain, making the command and control of units difficult. The center of the First Army lay on low ground with exten-

Air power was an important tool in the reduction of the German defenses in France prior to June 6. Allied military leaders had learned the hard way in North Africa that complete air superiority was going to be critical to the success of Operation Overlord. To accomplish this goal, the Luftwaffe had to be destroyed. Between January and June 1944, Allied fighter pilots accounted for 2,262 German fighter pilots and planes. One of the fighter planes that accounted for so many German planes was the famous P-51B Mustang, pictured here over Europe. *Real War Photos*

Before the Allies could break out of their small bridgehead in Normandy, Bradley's First Army had to punch out of the hedgerows that dominate so much of the area. The hedgerows date back centuries and were planted by French farmers to enclose their land. Most of the fields enclosed by hedgerows are fairly small, about 200 by 400 yards and irregular in shape. Pictured are American soldiers digging foxholes next to a hedgerow in Normandy. *Real War Photos*

sive marshlands. To make matters worse, the Germans had flooded most of the marshlands, restricting all wheeled and tracked vehicles to a few narrow roads. The right flank of the First Army faced a group of low hills dominating the northern end of the Cotentin Peninsula. These hills formed a natural defensive position on which the Germans anchored the western flank of their Normandy front.

Without question, the most important terrain obstacles faced by the First Army were the Normandy hedgerows. For centuries, Norman farmers followed the practice of enclosing their land with thick hedgerows. The French term for hedgerows is *Bocage,* meaning "grove." The American Army used the terms interchangeably. The hedgerows began right behind the original First Army landing beaches, and extended up to 50 miles inland in some areas. They made excellent defensive positions, providing cover and concealment to the German defenders and presenting a tough obstacle to the First Army attackers. The hedgerows restricted observation, making the effective use of tank guns or artillery almost impossible.

Feeling out each hedgerow for hidden German troops was a time-consuming process that could only be performed at close range. "Must go forward slowly, as we are doing," an American regimental commander wrote in a wartime

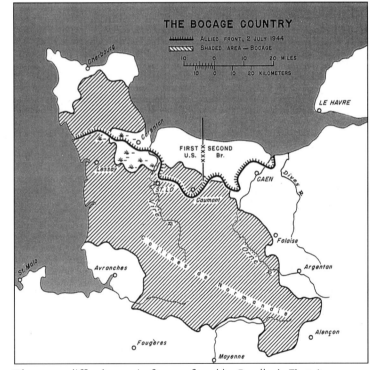

The most difficult terrain feature faced by Bradley's First Army was the Normandy hedgerows (also known by the French term the Bocage). The compartmentalized nature of the hedgerows made them a natural defensive position that the Germans took full advantage of throughout the fighting. The abundant vegetation and ubiquitous trees provided effective camouflage, obstructed observation, and hindered the employment of both artillery and tanks. *U.S. Army map*

The Normandy hedgerows come in no logical pattern. They are connected to one another by small, narrow trails that over the years turned into sunken lanes covered by overhead vegetation. The thick vegetation provided the Germans with excellent camouflage, hiding them from the view of American soldiers and tanks. Pictured are two German soldiers preparing for an American attack in Normandy. Both soldiers are equipped with the bolt-operated Mauser 98K, the standard shoulder weapon of the German Army. *Patton Museum*

The most successful method devised by the First Army to bash through hedgerows was developed by Sergeant Curtis G. Culin of the 2nd Armored Division. He designed and supervised the construction of a hedgerow-cutting device, as seen on this American M-5 light tank. The device was made from scrap iron mounted on the lower front hull of tanks. By late July 1944, over 60 percent of the First Army's tanks mounted the hedgerow-cutting devices. *National Archives*

ing for 20 years." A First Army wartime report stated, "Too many hedges and not the enemy, was the real deterrent to rapid advance."

Unable to outflank German hedgerow positions, American soldiers had to find ways to restore tactical mobility and to bring larger weapons to bear against the Germans. Many different methods saw use in an effort to allow tanks to cut through hedgerows. Some American units employed newly introduced "dozer" tanks, which consisted of standard M-4 Sherman tanks equipped with blades similar to those found on civilian bulldozers. Early experience in Normandy showed that a dozer tank could push its way through the largest hedgerows. Unfortunately for the First Army, there were not enough dozer tanks in Normandy to support large-scale operations. Some units used demolitions to blow gaps in the hedgerows large enough to drive through an M-4 Sherman. The technique proved workable but required more explosives than were readily available.

The best-known solution to the hedgerow problem came from Sergeant Curtis Culin of the 2nd Armored Division's 102nd Cavalry Reconnaissance Squadron. Sergeant Culin welded steel prongs to the front of Allied tanks, allowing the tanks to dig in and uproot a portion of the hedges. The prongs were hastily welded up from steel girders that had been part of the German beach defenses. Bradley saw the Culin hedgerow cutter on July 14 and ordered it

report. "Take one hedgerow at a time and clean it up." This was the standing operating procedure for the First Army for much of early July 1944. At this slow rate, many units could clear only a single hedgerow of the enemy in a day. Many First Army troops "could see the war last-

Crashing their way through hedgerows with the Culin device, American tanks would then use their weapons to suppress German machine gun positions. With the German machine guns silenced, American infantry would flush out any remaining German troops with small arms and grenades. Pictured are two American soldiers entering a hedgerow, opened up by a Culin hedgerow-cutting-equipped tank. In front of the American soldiers are two German soldiers who died defending their position.
Real War Photos

mass produced. Within 48 hours, Army Ordnance units built 500 of these makeshift hedgerow cutters. Enabling tanks to open passageways through the hedgerows, the "Culin Cutters" played an important role in the breakout from Normandy.

With the problems of armored mobility largely solved, infantry commanders could finally use the firepower of their supporting M-4 Sherman tanks. The tanks could now place heavy suppressive fire on the Germans, allowing Allied units a chance to maneuver. Properly employed, the machine guns of an M-4 Sherman delivered the direct fire needed to suppress German infantry fire, while the tank's main gun, used at pointblank range, substituted for indirect artillery fire.

As the tanks suppressed the German

defenders, American infantry units could clear out the hedgerows and maneuver to assault the main German defensive positions. The infantry could also provide tanks with protection against German counterattacks. Other improvisations, like external telephones on the rear decks of the tanks and infantry-frequency radios inside the tanks, increased the Americans' ability to fight as tank-infantry teams.

In the Allied grand plans for the invasion of France, little thought was given to the difficulty of fighting in the Normandy hedgerows. The planners for Operation Overlord had incorrectly assumed that the German forces in Normandy would retreat behind the Seine River near Paris when confronted with a successful Allied landing. As a result, Bradley's First Army was badly unprepared for the difficulties faced,

Over the centuries the Normandy hedgerows grew into sturdy embankments, half earth and half hedge. At their base they are as much as 4 feet thick with vegetation equally as thick growing to heights of almost 15 feet in spots. They made excellent defensive positions that the Germans took full advantage of whenever possible. Pictured is an American soldier firing a .30-caliber Browning machine gun through a hedgerow at German defensive positions. *Real War Photos*

and suffered horrible losses. The 90th Infantry Division lost 150 officers and 2,135 enlisted men in June, figures that would double in the following month.

Like the terrain, the weather also affected the operations in the Normandy campaign. More than anything else, constant rains during June and July hampered the efforts of the First Army. The early summer of 1944 was the wettest since 1900. The marshlands of Normandy turned into muddy swamps that swallowed men and equipment. Low visibility and cloud ceilings deprived ground units of fighter-bomber support and the aerial observers they needed. Additionally, a major storm struck the invasion beaches between June 19 and 22, severely restricting the movement of supplies onto the mainland. As a result, shortages of key supplies such as ammunition hampered operations during the battles in the hedgerows.

Patton's Arrival and the First Army's Plans

In the weeks following the invasion and before his arrival in Normandy, Patton's biggest concern was that the war would end before he had a chance to take part. Patton wrote in his diary, "I have a feeling, probably unfounded, that neither Monty (nickname for General Montgomery) nor Bradley are too anxious for me to have a command. If they knew what little respect I have for the fighting ability of either of them, they would be even less anxious for me to show them up."

The primary weapon employed by the Germans fighting in the hedgerows was the machine gun. Backing up the machine guns, the Germans used preplanned artillery and mortar fire. German mortar fire was particularly effective in Normandy, and accounted for 75 percent of all American front-line casualties. Pictured is a German 81-mm mortar team in action. The German 81-mm mortar weighed 125 pounds and had a range up to 2,625 yards. It was designated the 8-cm model in 1943. *Patton Museum*

With the Germans well concealed in the Normandy hedgerows, Bradley's First Army made little progress in the weeks following the initial landings. Bradley estimated that it took an average of five Americans to displace one German defender. During normal military offensive operations, it is commonly accepted that a ratio of three attackers to one defender will result in success for the attackers. Pictured in the Normandy hedgerows is an American Army 81-mm mortar M1 squad in action. *Real War Photos*

In the original invasion plans, the Third Army should have been in Normandy by June 16. As is the case in most military campaigns, however, the plans for Operation Overlord proved to be too optimistic. Patton finally flew to Normandy on July 6, in a C-47 transport plane escorted by P-47 fighters. His personal transport plane landed on an airfield very close to Omaha beach where, one month prior, Allied troops stormed ashore.

Patton's Third Army headquarters staff traveled to Normandy in a U.S. Navy landing ship tank (LST), arriving on the same day as their boss. Headquarters for the Third Army were set up in an apple orchard about 10 miles behind the First Army's front lines. Between August 1944, and the end of the war in May 1945, Patton's headquarters would move 19 more times.

Eisenhower ordered no publicity on Patton or the Third Army's arrival in Normandy. The Germans still firmly believed that Patton and his phantom 1st Army Group were ready to invade Pas de Calais and that the landings at

Prior to the invasion of France, the American Army guessed that it would incur losses of roughly 70 percent in its front-line units. By August, the fighting in the hedgerows had pushed losses up to 83 percent in the front-line units. Casualties among infantry officers were particularly high in the hedgerows, where small-unit initiative and individual leadership figured so greatly. Pictured is a First Army casualty station in Normandy. *Real War Photos*

Normandy were a diversion from the main assault yet to come. As long as this deception maintained itself, the Germans would keep many of their divisions immobile in the 15th Army sector and away from the fighting in Normandy.

Following Patton and his headquarters staff to Normandy were three of his four corps headquarters. The XV Corps headquarters arrived in Normandy on July 15. The XX Corps headquarters followed on July 24. The XII Corps headquarters involved itself with helping the Third Army units get from England to Normandy. It then helped them move off the original invasion beaches into the lodgment area. Part of the XII Corps headquarters reached Normandy on July 29, the remainder on August 7. To give close air support to the Third Army, Brigadier General Otto P.

Weyland's XIX Tactical Air Command (TAC) also moved from England to Normandy. Weyland's headquarters staff set up very close to Third Army headquarters.

With Cherbourg securely under First Army control, Bradley prepared his forces to advance southward once more. Bradley's orders, as received from Montgomery on the last day of June, were twofold. The first part involved continuing the expansion of the lodgment area, while the second part involved drawing German forces away from the British sector of Normandy by beginning offensive operations against the German Seventh Army. If Bradley's July offensive achieved all its goals, the First Army would be facing eastward toward Paris, and its right flank would be near the entrance into Brittany. At this point in the operation, Patton's Third Army was to become operational

Together in France, General George C. Marshall (Army Chief of Staff) and Patton pause for a photograph. As Marshall rose up the army ladder of command in the interwar years, he kept notes on officers who impressed him and that he thought could be suitable for future high-ranking positions in the Army. Patton had made a very favorable impression on Marshall in World War I. Marshall liked Patton personally, and thought of him as the best tank officer in the Army. It was Marshall who kept Patton in the Army, when other officers his age were being retired prior to America's entrance into World War II. *Patton Museum*

and move south and west to seize Brittany and its many ports. Once the Brittany ports were in American hands, the Third Army would be free to turn east to join Bradley's First Army. The First Army, in conjunction with the British and Canadian forces on its left, would, in the meantime, be advancing eastward to the Seine River and Paris.

During the early stages of fighting in the Normandy hedgerows, the infantry divisions of the First Army could not get the artillery support they wanted. The problem was the flat hedgerow thickets that blocked the view of ground-based forward artillery observers. To overcome this problem, the First Army began to depend on aerial artillery observers. The observers were flown over the battlefield in small L-4 Piper Cubs, as pictured, or the larger L-5 Stinson Sentinels. During the Normandy battles, aerial observers conducted the majority of artillery fire support missions. *National Archives*

Military Police (MP) units existed at army, corps, and divisional levels. The MP began the war with slightly more than 2,000 men in 1941. By the end of the war, it had more than 200,000 men. MPs performed a number of important jobs, such as directing traffic, guarding prisoners, and protecting important roads, bridges, and tunnels. It was also the job of the military police to maintain the internal security of headquarters units, as well as defend them in case of an enemy attack. *National Archives*

An important goal of the planned First Army July offensive was the high ground around the town of Coutances roughly 20 miles inland from the existing First Army positions. As things turned out, the First Army had to settle for something far short of its original goal. Heavy rains delayed Bradley's offensive operation until July 3. When the operation finally got off the ground, it began with three of Bradley's First Army corps advancing on a broad front. When they began moving forward, they quickly ran into heavy German resistance.

An intermediate objective of the First Army's drive southward was to capture the high ground around the town of Saint-Lo and the road outside the town that led to Coutances. Saint-Lo was an important road center as well as a German communications center. Like spokes on a wheel, roads ran in almost every direction from Saint-Lo. The military force that could control the city would control much of the road network in the hedgerow area of Normandy. The Germans were well aware of the city's strategic value. The defense of the city and the surrounding heights were entrusted to the veterans of Germany's II Parachute Corps.

The biggest roadblock to the advance of the First Army was its inability to support its infantry units with direct-fire weapons when assaulting hedgerows. Tanks could not climb over or through the hedgerows without exposing their weaker hull armor to German antitank fire. To overcome this problem, the Americans had to devise something that would allow tanks to bash through hedgerows. The first attempts at penetrating the hedgerows involved the use of specially equipped "dozer" tanks. The dozer tanks proved effective, but they were in short supply. *National Archives*

By the end of the first week of the invasion, Eisenhower's forces had consolidated a bridgehead 8 to 12 miles deep and about 50 miles long. Behind the front lines, Allied supply units tried to built up sufficient amounts of fuel, food, and ammunition to make possible the next phase of the attack to break out of the beachheads. Pictured is a British soldier guarding two Luftwaffe Field Division soldiers captured in battle. *Patton Museum*

The original Allied invasion plans called for the capture of Saint-Lo by June 16. The First Army's 29th Infantry Division launched an attack to capture the town on June 15. Some of the toughest fighting of the Normandy campaign took place around Saint-Lo for the next three days. The American division managed to get within five miles of the town, but no farther.

The British Role

In contrast to the difficult terrain fought in by Bradley's First Army, Montgomery's British Second Army sector was a relatively open, flat, and dry expanse. It stretched from the old French university town of Caen to Paris, 120 miles away. This made the area nearly perfect for the use of armored units and building airfields. British forces had planned on the capture of Caen, which lay about 10 miles inland from the British invasion beaches, on June 6. Due to stiff German resistance, Caen did not fall into British hands until July 10.

Once the Allies made their successful landing in Normandy, Hitler and his generals convinced themselves that Paris was the primary objective. The Germans felt that the British Second Army would carry the main weight of the Allied advance. They further surmised that the American First Army would fulfill only a secondary role in protecting the western flank of the British advance. Consequently, most of the best German units, especially the panzer divi-

The command of all Allied Ground Forces in Operation Overload went to General (later Field Marshal) Bernard Law Montgomery in December 1943. Montgomery continued to serve under Eisenhower's direction as Supreme Commander. On September 1, 1944, Eisenhower replaced Montgomery as commander of all field operations. Montgomery retained control of the 21st Army Group, which included both British and Canadian Armies. A British soldier prepares to drop a round down the tube of his 3-inch mortar. The British 3-inch mortar fired a 10-pound round. *National Archives*

sions, sat concentrated against Montgomery's Second British Army during most of the Normandy campaign.

At the end of June, the Second British Army, with a force equivalent to 16 divisions, was holding a front approximately 33 miles long. Along a 20-mile stretch of this front, the Germans concentrated seven armored divisions and elements of an eighth. Only two infantry divisions faced the extreme left flank of the British forces. By drawing the bulk of the German forces to their sector, the British and Canadians made possible the eventual breakout of American forces from Normandy in late July and August 1944.

First Army's Advance Ends

After much effort and heavy loss of life on both sides, Bradley's July offensive ground to a halt on July 19. Saint-Lo, now a complete ruin, came under American control the day before, but would remain under German mortar and artillery fire for another week. The road outside Saint-Lo that led to Coutances remained in German hands. In some areas, the First Army had advanced less than four miles. In that time, it had suffered more than 40,000 casualties, of which 90 percent were infantrymen. In the 15 days of fighting around Saint-Lo, the 30th Infantry Division alone had suffered 3,934 casualties.

In early July, Bradley launched the First Army at the French town of Coutances. Due to stiff German resistance and heavy rains, the American advance was both painfully slow and costly. Bradley soon lowered his sights on trying to seize the important road and rail center of Saint-Lo. During the heavy fighting for Saint-Lo the Germans employed elements of 12 divisions, including two armored divisions. Pictured is a column of American soldiers passing a destroyed German Panther tank near Saint-Lo. *Real War Photos*

There was a deep sense of disappointment shared by Bradley and other First Army commanders in their failure to capture Coutances. As the First Army regrouped for a new attempt, there was little realization that the July offensive had actually achieved some significant results, the most important of these being the wearing down of German forces in Normandy.

By July 17, German casualties in Normandy amounted to about 100,000 men, of which 2,360 were officers. The Germans could replace only about 12 percent of these casualties. Additionally, the Germans lost hundreds of tanks and other hard-to-replace equipment. Another serious problem created by the First Army's July offensive was Germany's inability to build up a

German paratroopers operate an 8-cm (81-mm) mortar outside Saint-Lo. The paratroopers are wearing the helmets and camouflage smocks unique to their organization. In a July 1944 report, American soldiers described German paratroopers as "Elite troops, with an unshakable morale; they asked no quarter and made certain that they gave none. . . ." *Patton Museum*

In a brutal and bloody advance through the Normandy hedgerows, First Army troops captured Saint-Lo on July 18. Pictured is an American infantryman looking over the body of a German soldier who died defending the outskirts of Saint-Lo. A survivor of the hedgerow fighting stated, "We won the battle of Normandy, [but] considering the high price in American lives, we lost." *Real War Photos*

An American supply convoy passes through what remains of Saint-Lo after its capture. Allied and German shelling and Allied aerial bombing reduced Saint-Lo to ruins. The Germans also suffered heavy casualties in men and equipment during the fighting for Saint-Lo. Unlike the Americans, the German remained hard-pressed to replace their losses. The result was the wearing down of their last immediate reserves for use against the upcoming American breakthrough. *Real War Photos*

strategic reserve, upon which any hope of a serious German counterattack against a possible Allied breakout from Normandy depended. The divisions brought in from other areas to build up a reserve found themselves committed piecemeal into battle to stop the First Army, as well as the British and Canadian, offensive operations.

Bradley and the other Allied leaders were not really aware just how close the German forces in Normandy had come to complete disintegration by mid-July. Generalfeldmarschall Guenther von Kluge, commander of all German Forces in France, was well aware of the serious difficulties facing his men. On July 13, Kluge called Generaloberst Alfred Jodl, chief of operations of the German Army, at Hitler's headquarters. Kluge wanted more tanks to stiffen the infantry units, which he feared could not hold on much longer. Kluge also asked Jodl to tell Hitler that the Normandy situation was "very serious." Kluge's warning went unheeded, however, and it proved accurate when Operation Cobra broke through German defensive lines a few weeks later.

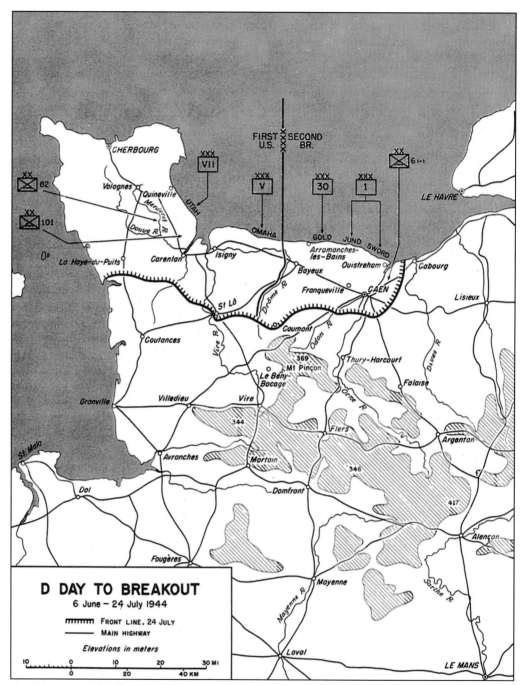

On July 24, the depth of the Allied beachhead was not much greater in July than it had been in June. There was not enough room in the area secured by the Allies since June 6 to bring in more divisions from England. The Allies needed room to maneuver their units, build airfields, and also acquire French seaports to ease the supply bottleneck, caused by bringing all supplies across the original landing beaches. *U.S. Army map*

Chapter Two

PATTON AND OPERATION COBRA

As early as 1942, top Allied military planners began to envision a major advance southward into Brittany and then eastward to Paris following the successful landing in Normandy. Both the terrain and military considerations, such as the French road network, favored such an operation. A major advance due south from Saint-Lo toward the Loire River and a turning movement to the east at the base of the Cotentin Peninsula would have numerous advantages. Such an attack would cut off the Germans in the Brittany peninsula. It would also give the Allied armies advancing on Paris a secure right flank on the Loire River, and allow the Allies to force the Germans back against the Seine River. The Germans would have to retreat northward through hilly country lying between British forces in the north and the U.S. forces in the south instead of using a more favorable southward escape route. A retreat southward would allow the Germans to join with their units in southern France or in the Alsace region of France.

Shortly before D-Day, the staff of Montgomery's 21st Army Group, with Eisenhower's approval, formalized plans for a major advance on Brittany and then an eastward drive toward Paris. Bradley's First Army received the assignment. Before the First Army could begin a major advance that would eventually take it eastward toward Paris and the Seine River, it had to break out of the Normandy hedgerows. When Bradley initially launched his First Army southward toward Coutances, he foresaw a quick collapse of the German lines. This expectation stemmed from overconfidence in American military strength and misleading intelligence reports. According to many of these reports, German units facing the First Army

The standard weapon of the American infantryman in World War II was the .30-caliber M-1 Garand. The well-known Garand was a semiautomatic gas-operated weapon weighing 9 1/2 pounds, with an internal magazine that held eight rounds. A trained soldier could fire eight well-aimed shots in about 20 seconds. By the end of the war American factories turned out more than 5 1/2 million Garands. *National Archives*

suffered from both poor morale and serious shortages of men and equipment. This information may have been true during the last week of June, but it was no longer accurate by the first week of July. In that short time the German units facing the First Army had become reorganized, resupplied, and strengthened. These rebuilt German units blunted Bradley's July 3 offensive operation.

On July 11, a German panzer division (the Panzer Lehr Division) launched a major counterattack against the XIX Corps of Bradley's

The crew of a camouflaged American antiaircraft gun scans the sky in all directions looking for any sign of German aircraft. Hidden under the bundles of straw is a Multiple .50-caliber machine gun carriage M-51. It consisted of a generator-powered one-man armored turret, mounting four .50-caliber machine guns. The powered turret was mounted on a four-wheel trailer that was towed into position. *National Archives*

An American Army Signal Corps photographer stares at a German soldier killed trying to use a Panzerschreck. The Panzerschreck (armor terror) was a weapon that would take a heavy toll on Allied tanks in Normandy. It was a shoulder-fired antitank rocket launcher employed by German infantry units, and its design was based on a captured American-made bazooka. The Germans made their version of the bazooka much larger and more powerful than the original American version. *National Archives*

Another infantry antitank weapon employed by the Germans was the Panzerfaust (armor fist). The first version of the Panzerfaust entered production in October 1943. It proved to be the world's first disposable, recoilless, one-man antitank weapon. Later versions had larger warheads and longer range. Pictured in the hands of an American officer is a captured Panzerfaust. *Patton Museum*

On July 11, the Germans launched the elite Panzer Lehr Armored Division in a counterattack against the First Army. Standing in the way of this crack German armored division were the American 9th and 30th Infantry Divisions. The Americans aimed every weapon they had at the advancing German tanks. Suffering heavy losses in their advance, the German tankers decided to withdraw from the battlefield. Pictured is a 45-ton Panther tank (model A) destroyed during the Panzer Lehr attack. The German Panther tank had a five-man crew and was armed with a high-velocity 75-mm gun. *Patton Museum*

First Army. Alerted by Magic/Ultra information, the First Army troops managed to repel the German attackers by that evening. Despite Magic/Ultra's valuable information to Bradley, the unexpectedly heavy German resistance facing the First Army in early July created an ever-increasing fear among top Allied leaders of an apparent military stalemate in Normandy. They considered a number of options to overcome this possibility, including an amphibious or airborne landing behind German lines. For various reasons, however, these options proved unattractive. Instead, it fell to Bradley on July 11 to come up with an acceptable concept to end the Normandy stalemate. Two days later, the First Army adopted one of Patton's ideas (without giving him credit) that became known as Operation Cobra.

The Cobra Buildup

Eisenhower enthusiastically received Bradley's plan, which called for a concentrated ground offensive along a very narrow front supported by a massive amount of air power. This type of ground offensive was a fairly novel concept for the Americans. U.S. Army doctrine, as favored by Eisenhower and Bradley throughout the war, encouraged a broad-front strategy, attacking the enemy forces simultaneously all along their front lines. Eisenhower knew from the Magic/Ultra information that the Germans disliked having to deal with an enemy approaching on a broad front. Nevertheless, the

Typical of the German tanks employed against the Allied armies in Normandy was the 23-ton Mark IV (H) medium tank, shown here. The Mark IV was the standard combat vehicle of most tank battalions in German armored divisions. Early models of the tank were developed before World War II, and later models of the Mark IV were both upgunned and uparmored. The Mark IV (H) model had a five-man crew and came armed with a high-velocity 75-mm gun. *Patton Museum*

perceived lack of success of Bradley's first offensive that had been conducted on a broad front had a large influence on the decision to adopt the narrow front proposed by Cobra.

Operation Cobra, from the beginning, was designed only as a limited attack. Its main purpose was to drive a hole in the German defenses west of Saint-Lo. If that breakthrough worked,

By the third week in July, Bradley's First Army was in position to launch an all-out attack to break through and destroy the German divisions, then attempt to contain them in the original beachhead area. To assist the First Army, Allied military leaders decided to employ air power on a massive scale never attempted before to support the ground attacks. Pictured is the crew of a Boeing B-17G Flying Fortress bomber named "Button Nose," reviewing maps prior to a bombing mission over France. *Real War Photos*

a deeper penetration into enemy territory by a large armored force would follow, thrusting deep into the German's rear, toward Coutances. When, and if, Coutances fell into the First Army's hands, Operation Cobra would end and be replaced by another operation aimed at the southern base of the Cotentin Peninsula, the gateway to Brittany.

With the capture of Coutances, Bradley originally foresaw implementing a holding action (in military terms known as a "consolidation phase"). During the holding action, the VII Corps would mop up any remaining German resistance and begin preparation for another follow-up operation. As events unfolded during Operation Cobra, Bradley's consolidation phase proved unnecessary.

While Operation Cobra plans developed, Montgomery remained in control of all ground operations in Normandy. He, in turn, allowed Bradley considerable freedom relative to plans for the First Army's operations. Eisenhower and his staff shipped additional units to Normandy and sped up deliveries of ammunition and supplies.

The First Army had four corps comprising 15 divisions on the army front. For additional

When and if Bradley's First Army achieved a breakthrough of the German lines, it was to swing armored spearheads westward to Coutances. This westward movement would isolate the German divisions between Saint-Lo and the coast. Once this goal was accomplished, they were then to strike down through Avranches, creating if possible another opening in the German lines. Pictured is an American M-4 Sherman tank in France being directed to an assembly area. *National Archives*

By capturing Coutances and creating an opening in the German lines, the First Army could then advance into the Brittany Peninsula to open up the much-needed ports. At the same time, the German Seventh Army and at least part of Panzer Group West could be encircled and crushed between the American forces to the West and the British and Canadians to the East. The damage to the front of this derelict German Army SdKfz 231 eight-wheel armored reconnaissance car indicates it hit a mine and was probably stripped for useable parts. *National Archives*

192764

Pictured together in Normandy are Montgomery and Bradley, during a rare meeting. Montgomery was very fond of small animals, and kept a number of them throughout the war. Patton heartily disliked Montgomery, and often belittled his skill as a general and his conduct of the Normandy campaign. Bradley, in contrast, thought very highly of Montgomery in the first months of the Normandy campaign. Beginning in August 1944, Bradley's relationship with Montgomery began to sour. By the end of the war, Bradley would become one of Montgomery's most bitter critics. *National Archives*

backup, the First Army could call upon an additional infantry division and two armored divisions. Patton's Third Army and several corps headquarters waited to become operational behind Bradley's First Army. For added assistance, the First Army employed many supporting units that belonged to the Third Army. These supporting detachments included engineer units, tank destroyer units, quartermaster units, evacuation hospitals, fuel supplies, truck companies, and graves-registration units.

During the early planning stages of Operation Cobra, Bradley told Eisenhower that he preferred to conduct the upcoming operation without Patton's Third Army. It was not until July 28 that Bradley decided to give Patton some part in Cobra prior to the activation of his Third Army on August 1. Bradley directed Patton to begin forming the six divisions of the First Army's VIII Corps into two separate corps. He also told Patton to keep track of these corps during the opening stages of Cobra, so that Patton would be familiar with the tactical situation when his army became operational. The other

Each 12-man American infantry squad had as standard equipment a single .30-caliber Browning Automatic Rifle (BAR) Model 1919A2. The gas-operated BAR weighed almost 20 pounds, and fired from a 20-round detachable box magazine. The BAR was far from a perfect squad support weapon. The 20-round magazine and the lack of a changeable barrel prevented any form of sustained fire. Despite these shortcomings, it was well liked by most American infantrymen who appreciated its knockdown power. *National Archives*

To distract German attention from the First Army's planned attack, Montgomery launched his 21st Army Group in a large offensive operation code-named "Goodwood" on July 18. On the following day, the plan called for Bradley to launch Operation Cobra near Saint-Lo in order to break through German defenses. Pictured is British infantry riding into battle on American-supplied M-4 Sherman tanks. *British Army Tank Museum*

Montgomery had high hopes that Operation Goodwood would not only distract German attention from Bradley's planned offensive, but punch a hole in the German defensive lines opposing his forces. At this point, Montgomery was under a great deal of pressure from both the Americans and his own government for some type of victory in Normandy. Unfortunately for Montgomery, the plans for Operation Goodwood were badly flawed and resulted in heavy losses in tanks and infantry. Pictured is a long column of British infantry on the move in France. *Patton Museum*

A British Army Universal Carrier in a French field. The Universal Carrier, often incorrectly referred to as a "Bren Gun Carrier," originally appeared in British Army service before World War II began. The English-built Universal Carrier was merely an improved model, based on the Bren Carrier design. Within Montgomery's 21st Army Group, the Universal Carrier saw use in many different roles, including armored personnel carrier and mortar carrier. *British Army Tank Museum*

three corps that made up the First Army would remain under the command of General Courtney H. Hodges, assistant commander of the First Army.

As the number of divisions grew and preparations continued for the activation of Patton's Third Army, it became more difficult for First Army headquarters to effectively direct all the various military forces in Normandy. On July 19, Bradley recommended that the First and Third Armies be commanded by an army group headquarters. Allied planners for the invasion of France had foreseen such a need, and on July 25, Eisenhower approved Bradley's suggestion. Eisenhower directed that all American ground forces in Normandy be regrouped into the First and Third Armies under the control of the 12th Army Group, which Bradley was to command. Bradley chose August 1 for the new command arrangement to go into effect. Hodges succeeded Bradley as commander of the First Army.

GERMAN AND AMERICAN DIVISIONAL ORGANIZATION

Despite the common belief that the German ground forces were primarily an armored force, they were, in reality, an infantry force that depended on its feet and horses for movement. The typical German infantry division had almost 5,000 horses. Of the roughly 300 divisions available to Germany in July 1944, only 33 were panzer divisions, whereas the remaining divisions were mostly infantry. The others consisted of Waffen SS and Luftwaffe (German Air Force) field divisions, including parachute divisions.

Due to the dwindling manpower supply, the German Army scaled back its standard infantry divisions in early 1944, resulting in the so-called 1944 type of infantry division of 12,769 men. The new smaller divisions either had three regiments with two rifle battalions, or two regiments with three battalions. Despite Germany's attempts to standardize its infantry divisions, there remained exceptions to the rule. Certain German Army divisions, as well as Waffen SS infantry divisions and Luftwaffe parachute divisions, remained much larger than their Army 1944 type of infantry division counterparts, with as many as 22,000 men.

Unlike the more numerous and fairly standard German infantry divisions of 1944, no two German armored divisions in France had the same strength and structure. Personnel strength in the armored divisions ranged from 12,768 to 21,386 men. The maximum tank strength of a German armored division on paper consisted of roughly 190 tanks. In reality, German armored divisions seldom were at full strength. Between June 6 and July 17, the German armored divisions in Normandy lost about 240 tanks and yet received only 17 replacement vehicles. In addition to tank formations, German armored divisions contained mechanized infantry, self-propelled artillery units, anti-tank vehicles, reconnaissance detachments, and repair and maintenance units.

Like the German Army, the bulk of the American Army consisted of infantry divisions. Unlike the German Army, however, the American infantry divisions moved primarily on wheels. Each infantry division had roughly 2,000 vehicles of all types. Yet despite this large number, most infantrymen still walked to battle.

The American infantry divisions that went ashore into Normandy were "triangular" divisions of roughly 14,000 men each. By 1945, the American Army had formed 68 triangular infantry divisions, of which 42 fought in the northwest European campaign. The basic composition of the triangular division was three infantry regiments, each of which consisted of three infantry battalions of 871 men each. The infantry battalions received support from a variety of combat and combat-support troops at the regiment and division level. If these combat and combat-support units had been combined, the U.S. Army would have had an additional four infantry divisions. Each infantry battalion was further divided into three rifle companies and a weapons company.

Rifle companies consisted of three rifle platoons, a weapons platoon, and a small headquarters section, with a total manpower strength of six officers and 187 enlisted men. The weapons platoon was armed with two .30-caliber and one .50-caliber machine gun, three 60-mm mortars, and three 2.36-inch rocket launchers (bazookas).

Three infantry squads constituted a rifle platoon. In theory, each rifle squad consisted of 12 men armed with 10 .30-caliber M1 Garand rifles, 1 Browning automatic rifle (BAR), and either a .45-caliber submachine gun, M-1 carbine, or M-1903A3 rifle. Despite the many weapons within a triangular division, the lifeblood of the infantry division was the 5,211 officers and combat infantrymen who manned its 27 rifle companies. Four artillery battalions supported each triangular infantry division. These battalions consisted of three 105-mm howitzer battalions with 12 towed guns each, and a single 155-mm howitzer battalion with 12 towed guns.

Armor support for triangular infantry divisions came from nondivisional independent tank battalions. These units also were referred to as "general headquarters (GHQ) tank units." Sixty-five independent tank battalions were formed during World War II; roughly half of them served in the northwestern European campaign. A typical independent tank battalion consisted of a headquarters company, a service company, 3 medium tank companies of 17 tanks each, and a light tank company of 17 tanks.

In addition to independent tank battalions, the American Army fielded 16 armored divisions during World War II. If brought together, the 65 independent tank battalions were equal to an additional 21 armored divisions. Except for the 1st Armored Division, which served in North Africa and Italy, all of the armored divisions served in the northwestern European campaign. Fourteen of the 16 armored divisions had a new triangular organization, similar to the infantry divisions, implemented in September 1943. They had a total strength of slightly fewer than 10,000 men and 2,755 vehicles, 263 of which were tanks. These units were designated as light armored divisions.

Two armored divisions, the 2nd and 3rd, had been in England preparing for the invasion of France when the 1943 reorganization took place. The Army did not want to delay their battle readiness and left them with the original pre-1943 organization of more than 16,000 men and 310 tanks. These two units were referred to as heavy armored divisions.

Triangular armored divisions had three tank battalions. Each battalion consisted of a headquarters company, a service company, three medium tank companies of 17 tanks each, and a light tank company of 17 light tanks. Tank battalions normally operated as a complete unit. In addition to its three tank battalions, the triangular armored division had three battalions of armored infantry carried in half-tracks, and three battalions of self-propelled artillery. Many armored divi-

GERMAN AND AMERICAN DIVISIONAL ORGANIZATION (continued)

sions would occasionally borrow an infantry battalion from a nearby infantry division for certain operations. For combat operations, the various battalions of the triangular armored divisions were organized into "combat commands (CC)."

Other elements of the triangular armored division were its mechanized cavalry squadrons, armed with light tanks and armored cars, an engineer battalion, and the division train (supply and maintenance vehicles). The armored division had no organic tank destroyers or large antiaircraft weapons. It did have both antitank and antiaircraft weapons of lighter types. To supplement the armored division in combat, nondivisional units from corps and army pools were usually attached to an armored division on a semipermanent basis. These attached units generally included a tank destroyer battalion, an antiaircraft battalion, a 155-mm artillery battalion, quartermaster truck companies, a quartermaster gasoline supply company, and an engineer treadway bridge company.

Bradley was not at all happy that Patton was in command of the Third Army. In contrast to the colorful and autocratic Patton, Bradley was modest and retiring. Nevertheless, Bradley soon developed a special relationship with Patton that would last till the end of the war. As a result of this relationship, Bradley would not only protect Patton from Eisenhower's wrath, but he would often give Patton's Third Army priority over his other armies. After the war, Bradley wrote about his relationship with Patton, "He had not been my choice for Army commander and I was still wary of the grace with which he would accept our reversal in roles. I was apprehensive in having George join my command, for I feared that too much time would probably be spent in curbing his impetuous habits."

Operation Goodwood

To draw away German forces from the First Army's limited attack toward Coutances, Montgomery planned for the British Second Army to begin its own offensive operation toward Caen with the hope of rupturing German defense lines. The British advance on Caen, code-named

One of the most formidable threats faced by the tankers of Montgomery's 21st Army Group was the legendary Tiger tank. It came in two basic models, the Tiger I (pictured here), which entered service in August 1942, and the Tiger II, which replaced the Tiger I in production in August 1944. Both models of the Tiger tank had thick armor protection and a powerful 88-mm high-velocity gun. For the more lightly armed and armored tanks used by the Allies, the Tigers were practically indestructible. *British Army Tank Museum*

The only Allied tank to see service in Normandy that could consistently punch holes in German Tiger (or Panther) tanks was the Sherman "Firefly." The Firefly was armed with a high-velocity 17-pounder (76.2-mm) gun. The British-developed gun proved to be far superior in hitting power to the 75-mm and 76-mm guns mounted on American Sherman tanks. Due to a shortage of 17-pounder guns, only one British Sherman tank in four had one in Normandy. Pictured is a Canadian Army Sherman Firefly. *Patton Museum*

"Goodwood," began with a massive, 2,100-plane air strike on the German positions, followed by the Allies sending three armored divisions toward German lines east of Caen.

Operation Goodwood confirmed the German belief that the main Allied breakout lay in the British sector around Caen and not in the American sector. Unknown to the British planners of Operation Goodwood, the German defenses in the Caen area were organized in depth, with infantry forward and the tanks back, east of Caen. As British tanks advanced toward German tank units untouched by the massive Allied aerial bombardment, which had only affected the forward positions, they came under murderous antitank and tank-gun fire. The British pushed forward long after they had lost their initial momentum, losing 126 tanks in the first day. They lost another 200 tanks before turning back the German counterattack that ended Operation Goodwood on July 21. If Operation Goodwood had succeeded, it might not have been necessary for Bradley to launch Operation Cobra.

Operation Goodwood's lack of success did not stop Montgomery from ordering additional diversionary attacks to aid Operation Cobra. On the morning of July 25, a Canadian corps began an attack in the Caen area. The Canadian attack quickly bogged down under heavy German resistance and a large armored counterattack. The Canadians lost more than 1,500 men, and were unwilling to risk more. Montgomery called a halt to the attack the same day it had started. On July 30, Montgomery launched the Second British Army in an operation to prevent German armored reserves from being switched to the American sector.

Operation Cobra Unleashed

On the eve of Operation Cobra, Eisenhower wrote Bradley, "My high hopes and best wishes ride with you in the attack . . . which is the largest ground assault yet staged in the war by American troops exclusively. Speaking as the responsible American rather than the Allied Commander, I assure you that . . . a breakout at this juncture will minimize the total cost [of victory]. . . . Pursue every advantage with an ardor verging on recklessness and with all your troops, without fear of major counteroffensive from the [troops the] enemy now has on his front. . . . The results will be incalculable."

The original plans for Operation Cobra called for the attack to begin on July 18. Due to poor weather, however, Bradley had to postpone it until July 24. The area Bradley chose for the opening move was on the 4.2-mile front of Major General Joseph ("Lightning Joe") Lawton Collins' VII Corps consisting of six divisions: the 1st, 4th, 9th, and 30th Infantry Divisions, and the 2nd and 3rd Armored Divisions. The 9th, 4th, and 30th concentrated for the initial assault, with the others following closely

During the war, many 88-mm guns saw employment as antitank weapons. The 88-mm gun fired a 33-pound armor-piercing (AP) round, which easily punched holes in all Allied tanks. Throughout the war, American Army surveys among combat troops showed the 88-mm gun to be one of the most feared German weapons. Located somewhere in France, this destroyed 88-mm antiaircraft gun is being examined by an American soldier. *National Archives*

behind a massive aerial bombardment. If they could penetrate German lines, they would create a defended corridor only three miles wide.

Down this narrow defended corridor the VII Corps would push the 1st Infantry Division (supplied with extra trucks) as well as the 2nd and 3rd Armored Divisions. The three divisions were to act as an exploiting force and encircle and secure Coutances, disrupt German

An M-4 Sherman tank rolls off a U.S. Navy Landing Ship Tank (LST) onto Omaha beach. Weighing about 32 tons and crewed by five, the Sherman tank came in many different models and versions. Standard armament on most Shermans consisted of a low-velocity 75-mm gun and at least two machine guns. Later models featured a higher-velocity 76-mm gun. Neither the 75-mm nor the 76-mm proved able to punch holes in German late-war tanks such as the formidable Panther or Tiger. *Real War Photos*

defenses, and set up further exploitation. To protect the advance of the VII Corps, the job of the VIII, V, and XIX Corps was to tie down German forces that could counterattack an Operation Cobra breakthrough. Opposing the VII Corps in the initial assault were roughly 3,000 German soldiers and 100 tanks.

To assist in the assault, the First Army assembled one of the greatest concentrations of firepower in the European Theater of Operation during World War II. In conjunction with the massive air bombardment, American artillery played a critical role in the success of the initial breakthrough. More than 20 battalions of divisional and corps artillery were under the operational control of a single corps headquarters. The artillery pieces employed included everything from 240-mm howitzers to 105-mm howitzers.

The key to getting Cobra rolling and through German lines was the planned aerial bombardment by 2,500 planes that would begin 80 minutes before the ground attack. The bombardment was intended to saturate a German front-line area five miles long and one mile wide west of Saint-Lo with 5,000 tons of high explosives, napalm, and white phosphorus. The air strike was intended to severely disrupt, if not destroy, German communications as well as

Artillery also played an important role in assisting in the opening blows of Operation Cobra. Typical of the corps artillery pieces employed during the offensive included the 240-mm howitzer M-1. It weighed 28 tons when fully emplaced and fired a 360-pound shell to a top range of about 14 miles. Due to its size it had to be broken down into two pieces when transported. A 20-ton crane was needed to reassemble the pieces before it could be placed into action. *National Archives*

Another artillery piece to see heavy use during Operation Cobra was the 155-mm gun M-1. It quickly acquired the popular nickname of the "Long Tom" due to its very long barrel. The Long Tom fired a roughly 95-pound shell out to 25,715 yards. It was considered a medium gun, and was found at the corps level. Its primary mission lay in reinforcing divisional artillery units. *National Archives*

The attempted breakthrough by Bradley's First Army began on July 25, 1944. The attack was preceded at dawn, on that day, by what was the heaviest and most concentrated air assault ever employed in support of ground operations. Over 2,000 aircraft of the Royal Air Force (RAF) Bomber Command and the American Eighth and Ninth Air Forces took part, dropping a total of over 7,000 tons of bombs. Taken from an American bomber, this photo shows bombs dropping toward the Germans below. *Real War Photos*

The opening bombardment of Operation Cobra took a heavy toll on the tanks of the German panzer division facing the planned American breakthrough. Allied bombs overturned tanks, cut telephone wires, and buried men and equipment. Of the 100 tanks and tank destroyers the Germans had in the area bombed by the Allies, less than a dozen survived. Pictured is a German Mark IV medium tank that has suffered the type of damage inflicted by a large aerial bombardment. *National Archives*

create havoc within Germany's lines. Without communications systems, the Germans would have difficulty organizing a coordinated defense against the ground attack.

The actual aerial operation got off to a false start on July 24, when bad weather postponed the operation minutes before it was to begin. Due to communications problems, over 300 American planes failed to receive the cancellation messages and dropped their bombs on the assigned targets. Human error caused a number of bombs to drop short of their targets. These bombs landed on First Army positions, resulting in the deaths of 25 men and the wounding of another 131.

The false start of Operation Cobra caused many American military commanders, including Bradley, to fear they had lost the element of tactical surprise. But Eisenhower overruled any thoughts about postponing Operation Cobra. He was very eager to see the operation begin. With prospects for good weather the next day, Bradley reluctantly ordered that Operation Cobra be launched at 11 A.M. on July 25. Fortunately, the German commanders saw the July 24 air attack only as a ruse and did not drastically alter their defensive positions. When the real bombardment began the next day, the Germans were unprepared for the scope of the attack.

While RAF heavy bombers dropped over 5,000 tons of bombs in less than 45 minutes on the area in which the First Army ground assault was to be made, American planes attacked the German troop concentrations to the rear and on the flanks. At the same time, a strong naval bombardment was made to supplement the air effort. Pictured here are U.S. Navy personnel preparing to fire the main guns of their battleship at German targets in Normandy. *Real War Photos*

Within American armored divisions, the three battalions of armored infantry rode into battle on armored half-tracks. The version of the half-track to see service with the American Army in the greatest numbers was the M-3 series. The seating capacity of the M-3 half-track was 13 men, including a driver. Thinly armored and open-topped, the armored infantry that rode in them suffered heavy losses throughout the war. The M-3 half-track pictured has suffered heavy damage from an unknown weapon. Visible behind the destroyed half-track is a 57-mm antitank gun M-1 that was in tow. *National Archives*

The commander of a German armored division (Panzer Lehr), which took the brunt of the air assault, later said, "By noon, nothing was visible but dust and smoke. My front lines looked like the face of the moon and at least 70 percent of my troops were out of action—dead, wounded, crazed, or numbed. All my forward tanks were knocked out, and the roads were practically impassable." Roughly 1,000 German soldiers perished in the Cobra bombardment. Of the 100 operational tanks the German Army had available, fewer than a dozen survived the aerial bombardment. Some of the German soldiers in the bombardment area remained deaf 24 hours later.

Operation Cobra Picks up Steam

During the second Operation Cobra bombardment, human error once again caused bombs to fall short, hitting First Army units. More than 111 American troops died, with another 490 wounded. Among the Americans killed was Lieutenant General Lesley J. McNair, the commanding general of all Army ground forces.

As the three lead infantry divisions ad-

In 1944, every armored infantry rifle company had three towed 57-mm antitank gun M-1s. This same weapon was the standard antitank gun in all American infantry divisions. Sadly, the 57-mm antitank gun proved unable to punch holes in German tanks and therefore was seldom used in its intended role. Pictured at the side of a road, the crew of a 57-mm antitank gun awaits a German attack. In some units, including some in Patton's 6th Armored Division, all the 57-mm antitank guns were conveniently lost in the advance across France. *National Archives*

Although only temporary in effect, the results of the Allied bombing and shelling were decisive as far as the initial ground attack was concerned. Actual casualties to the German soldiers in their foxholes were comparatively few. The weight of the bombardment proved more effective in causing a high degree of confusion among the German defenders facing the First Army advance. Pictured are German soldiers taken prisoner by American soldiers. *National Archives*

At the divisional level, the largest artillery piece in service with the American Army in World War II was the 155-mm howitzer M-1. First introduced into service in 1942, the 155-mm howitzer M-1 fired a 95-pound shell out to a top range of 16,000 yards. It proved to be a dependable and robust piece of equipment, well liked by its crews. A later version of the howitzer was designated the M-1A1. The M-1 155-mm howitzer shown here has just been fired, and the barrel is in full recoil. *Real War Photos*

vanced into the German lines, some of the surviving German troops put up a spirited defense, which shocked and surprised the advancing American infantrymen who believed nothing could have survived the rain of bombs. The advance soon slowed and the divisions achieved none of the planned geographical objectives. A very disappointed Bradley wrote that he thought "there was little reason to believe we stood at the brink of a breakthrough. Rather, the attack looked as though it might have failed." Unbeknownst to Bradley and the other First Army commanders, the initial ground attack actually succeeded better than anyone had supposed. The VII Corps infantrymen continued to face fire from the enemy, which could be possible as long as even just a few survived.

"Lightning Joe" Collins noted that the remaining German defenses seemed to lack coordination. He knew that he needed to act before the Germans could refashion a new defensive line. He also remained concerned that the Germans were forewarned by the premature Allied bombing of July 24. The Germans could

Another feared weapon employed by the Germans in Normandy was the Nebelwerfer. The Nebelwerfer was a six-barreled rocket launcher that was fired from wheeled ground mounts or from the back of an armored half-track as shown. Due to the horrible noise the rounds generated in flight, Allied soldiers nicknamed them the "moaning minnie" or "screamin' meemies." *Patton Museum*

After the air and artillery bombardment the first wave of Bradley's troops, from the VII Corps, advanced on a three-divisional front west of Saint-Lo. The general objectives of the first wave were the towns of Marigny and Saint Gilles and the road that connected them to Coutances. Pictured are American infantrymen checking a hedgerow for German soldiers. Lying at the feet of the American soldier, in the foreground, is a dead German soldier. *Real War Photos*

In addition to the resistance offered by the remaining German soldiers in the path of the First Army attack, the American soldiers also ran into intense artillery fire from German defensive positions not neutralized by the air bombing on the left flank. On the right flank, German parachute units resisted fiercely. Pictured in this early war photo is a German 15-mm (150-mm) gun. This weapon was the standard German medium artillery gun in World War II. It fired a 96-pound shell out to 18,163 yards. *Patton Museum*

have withdrawn their main line, and escaped the full force of the aerial bombardment. They may have set up a new defensive line not yet apparent to him and be preparing a counterattack against his forces.

To "Lightning Joe" Collins, the million-dollar question revolved around a decision to commit the 2nd and 3rd Armored Divisions and the 1st Infantry Division. He quickly recognized that to attempt a breakthrough depended on getting through the German forward defensive lines as soon as possible. He could not wait for the 4th, 9th, and 30th Infantry Divisions to achieve their planned objectives of Marigny and Saint Gilles. Both towns lay astride the important road that connected Saint-Lo to Coutances, the capture of which was considered essential to continuing the armor advance of Cobra toward Coutances. Collins decided to take a chance and committed his exploiting force on the morning of July 26. Two hundred fighter-bombers were to attack each town in advance of Collins' armored thrusts. In addition

The German armored divisions that could have counterattacked the First Army advance remained tied down in front of Montgomery's 21st Army Group farther north. On the day Operation Cobra began, there were 645 German tanks facing Montgomery's forces and only 190 facing Bradley's First Army. Pictured here is a column of Canadian vehicles advancing past a destroyed German Panther tank. *Patton Museum*

to the VII Corps' advance, the VIII, V, and XIX Corps began their own advances on July 26.

Major General Edward H. Brooks, commanding the Second Armored Division, took Saint Gilles by the afternoon of the 26th. His division made good progress and, in fact, achieved the greatest penetration on the VII Corps front. At the same time, the 1st Infantry Division, with part of the 3rd Armored Division under Major General Clarence A. Huebner, attacked toward Marigny. Huebner had hoped to take Marigny quickly and then advance westward from Marigny to Coutances. Such an advance would cut off the German troops facing the VIII Corps on the right flank of the VII Corps. German commanders could see what was happening, however. They set up a strong defensive line facing Huebner's advance and began withdrawing their units.

Near Marigny, Huebner's troops ran into tough German resistance, including tanks of the Second SS Panzer Division. Despite Huebner's troops' best efforts, they could not get past the German defenses to capture Marigny. Not

Throughout World War II, the bulk of German ground forces depended on their feet to move around the battlefield. Heavier items, like artillery pieces, were pulled by large numbers of horses. The typical German infantry division had at least 5,000 horses in its inventory. Pictured is a captured German Army horse-drawn wagon being driven by an American soldier. In contrast to the German infantry divisions, the Allied armies that landed in Normandy were fully motorized. *National Archives*

Slowed down by German resistance, the first attack wave of the VII Corps proved unable to reach its planned objectives. It was then decided by the VII Corps commander that the attack must continue at all costs. Three more divisions of the VII Corps, including two armored divisions, were passed through the first wave, turned westward, and struck for Coutances. Pictured is a burned-out M-4A1 Sherman tank being dragged aboard the trailer of an M-26 "Dragon Wagon" tank recovery vehicle. *National Archives*

By turning his armored divisions westward, the VII Corps commander managed to cut off the German forces along the coast, opposite the VIII Corps of the First Army. The job of the VIII Corps, then under Patton's unofficial control, was to advance forward and crush the German forces trapped along the coast. American infantrymen from a passing armored column inspect a couple of abandoned German Volkswagen-type 82 military cars, the inferior German equivalent to the American jeep. *National Archives*

wanting to delay the armored advance on Coutances, Huebner sent part of the 3rd Armored Division down the road toward Coutances on the morning of the 27th. At the same time, the 1st Infantry Division managed to capture Marigny on the morning of the 27th. The remaining elements of the 3rd Armored Division were also committed to battle. The Third only managed to get halfway to Coutances on the 28th before being stopped by continuing heavy German resistance.

Bradley, taking advantage of an ever-changing situation, decided to reassign the capture of Coutances from the VII Corps to the VIII Corps. The 4th and 6th Armored Divisions captured Coutances on the afternoon of the 28th. The VII Corps had achieved only a disappointing and partial success. What they had done, however, was to attract German reserves to their area. Thus, when the VIII Corps under Major General Troy H. Middleton began its advance on the morning of July 26, it found little Ger-

On July 26, the First Army took both the towns of Marigny and Gilles, thereby cutting the road between Saint-Lo and Coutances. On the same day the VIII Corps attacked to the west of the VII Corps. The Germans continued to counterattack vigorously as the American VII Corps thrust swung westward toward Coutances. The Germans wanted to hold Coutances as long as possible in order to withdraw their troops from the north facing the advancing VIII Corps under Patton. Pictured is a long column of American armored infantrymen in their M-3 half-tracks passing through a French town. *National Archives*

man opposition. By the 27th, the Germans had also begun disengaging from the VII Corps front.

On July 28, part of the 2nd Armored Division drove southeast to cut off the German withdrawal. The 82nd Reconnaissance Battalion pushed through the defenses before the Germans were aware of what was going on and seized blocking positions south of Coutances. German opposition was eliminated by the combined arms team of tanks, infantry, artillery, and fighter-bombers. By the morning of July 30, the 2nd Armored Division had killed a total of 1,500 German troops as well as captured another 4,000; sustaining a loss of 100 of its own men killed and another 300 wounded.

News of the initial successes was slow in reaching Eisenhower, but he maintained that the men were fighting for all their worth and that the enemy would soon crack under the pressure. Impressed by the reported effects of bombing on enemy morale, he felt that a concerted, intensive drive could break through the whole enemy defense system on a selected front, and that the Allies were going "to get a great victory, very soon."

Patton Becomes a Player in Cobra

Originally envisioned as a limited break through the Saint-Lo area, Operation Cobra managed to achieve all of its goals by July 28, with the First Army's capture of Coutances.

On July 28, the German escape route through Coutances was sealed with the capture of the city by the Fourth Armored Division, which, together with the 6th Armored Division, formed the spearhead of the VIII Corps under Patton's command. The German withdrawal, following the loss of Coutances, quickly degenerated into a disorderly retreat. Pictured is an American M-4 Sherman tank passing through the captured town of Coutances. *National Archives*

While the 2nd Armored Division continued to carry out some of its original Operation Cobra objectives until July 30, all four corps of the First Army began carrying out Bradley's new orders to exploit the Operation Cobra results.

A much encouraged Bradley wrote in the official First Army report on July 28, "The ensuing period, which the plan had conceived would be a holding and mopping-up period, became a vigorous attack period." He also wrote to Eisenhower on the 28th to report, "that we are taking every calculated risk and we believe we have the Germans out of the ditches and in complete demoralization and expect to take full advantage of them."

Bradley ordered Patton, whose Third Army was scheduled to become operational at noon of August 1, to "supervise" the advance of Middleton's VIII Corps on the coastal flank. This command arrangement would establish a useful continuity between the exploitation of the Operation Cobra breakout and future operations in Brittany. Patton immediately took over the planning of the VIII Corps' advance. Even in his limited supervising role, he began to embellish the attack plan with his own brand of audacity. He withdrew his infantry spearheads and replaced them with two armored divisions, the 4th and the 6th. Patton once wrote: "The primary mission of armored units is the attacking of infantry and artillery. The enemy's rear is the happy hunting ground for armor; use every means to get it there."

The 6th Armored Division, attacking south along the coast, was to exert the main effort. It soon managed to advance more than eight miles a day against weak opposition. The main effort had now shifted from the VII Corps to

With the capture of Coutances and the end of Operation Cobra, Bradley had the VIII Corps, under Patton's control, continue southward toward Avranches, which was captured on July 30. By the next day there remained no effective German forces to slow down the planned advance of Patton's Third Army into Brittany. Pictured are two M-4 Sherman tanks, destroyed by German anti-tank fire, on the outskirts of Avranches. *National Archives*

the VIII Corps as the flow of the battle overtook the original Cobra plans. By the evening of July 28, the local German corps headquarters had lost effective control of its units. Most of the survivors were trying to escape to the Southeast. American fighter-bombers discovered a large traffic jam of fleeing German troops and destroyed more than 500 vehicles.

In the original plans for Operation Cobra, Coutances had been the pinnacle of success for Bradley's First Army. After its capture, and with the entire German Seventh Army on the run, Avranches had now become the primary objective of the First Army and Patton's soon-to-be-activated Third Army. Avranches was the gateway to Brittany and probably the only way out of Normandy for the remaining German forces.

On the 29th, Patton's 4th and 6th Armored Divisions began moving southward again with the aim of capturing Avranches. Another objective was the securing of the bridge four miles south of Avranches leading to Pontaubault. Part of the Fourth Armored Division advanced 18 miles on July 30 to capture Avranches, the vital point in the area for both attack and defense. On the late afternoon of July 31, a task force of the 4th seized the bridge leading to Pontaubault as well as the important road intersection immediately south of it despite some minor German resistance. Together, the 4th and 6th had taken more

Despite the disorganization brought on the Germans by the Operation Cobra air bombardment, enough German troops remained in the attack area to slow down the first wave of Bradley's troops. American soldiers were always impressed with the ability of German troops to hold on to a position under the most difficult conditions. Pictured walking into battle is the typical American infantryman, armed with an M-1 Garand rifle. *National Archives*

On August 1, Patton's Third Army was activated. Patton took over command of the VIII, XII, XV, and XX Corps, while V, VII, and XIX Corps remained with the First Army. The two armies were then placed under the command of Bradley's new 12th Army Group. Lieutenant General Courtney H. Hodges succeeded Bradley as commander of the First Army. Pictured together are a smiling Patton (right) and Bradley (center). Hodges, the new commander of the First Army, is on the left. *National Archives*

than 4,000 prisoners on July 31. The two infantry divisions following the armored divisions had taken an additional 3,000 prisoners. In contrast to these figures, the total casualty count for VIII Corps between July 28 and July 31 numbered fewer than 700 men.

The Operation Cobra breakthrough was complete and would now turn into a breakout.

For the Germans, the situation had become a *Riesensauerei* (giant pigpen). The commander of Germany's Seventh Army telephoned Hitler's headquarters on July 31 to say, ". . . if the Americans get through at Avranches they will be out of the woods and they'll be able to do what they want."

Chapter Three

PATTON'S THIRD ARMY ON THE OFFENSIVE

Hitler held an important conference with his staff in his East Prussian headquarters on July 31, where he confirmed that the success of Operation Cobra and a possible future breakout could eventually lead to the withdrawal of German forces in Normandy. Therefore, he ordered the organization of a special army staff to plan for a pullout if it became necessary. At the same time, he ordered that new defensive positions be built along the Somme and Marne Rivers.

In an effort to gain time, Hitler also insisted there be no withdrawing from the existing defensive lines. He expected all ground controlled by German forces to be held with fanatical determination. Hitler knew that if France fell, the Allied threat to Germany would become immediate. If the German Army High Command approved a withdrawal, all French roads, communication facilities, bridges, and railroads were slated for destruction in the wake of a German retreat. French ports were to be held to the last man and then destroyed before falling into Allied hands.

On July 29, Bradley, in his role as the future 12th Army Group commander, issued orders to Patton and his soon-to-be-activated Third Army to drive south from Pontaubault to seize the cities of Rennes and Forgeres, then turn westward to secure the various Breton ports, and finally to seize the remainder of Brittany. Bradley envisioned these goals being accomplished by Third Army armored and infantry divisions working together in an orderly advance, as had been done during the post-Operation Cobra drive to Avranches.

Patton saw little point in slowly reducing Brittany by carefully planned set-piece operations taking place in successive phases. He knew

the German forces within Brittany were weak. Patton even joked with his staff that he did not want the press to know just how second-rate his opponents were in Brittany.

Patton had already begun to see the conquest of Brittany as a secondary assignment even before he officially took command of the

The Germans successfully employed a large number of tanks in their quick conquest of Poland in 1939. This forced the American Army to reevaluate its ability to stop attacks by mass formations of German armor. By December 1941, eight antitank battalions were formed. At the time, they were renamed tank destroyer (TD) battalions because the term antitank was too passive sounding. An example of what the Army's TD program produced during the war is the M-10, as seen here with its happy crew hamming it up for the photographer. The M-10 had a crew of five and was armed with a 3-inch gun mounted in an open-topped, five-sided turret. *Patton Museum*

By 1944, Adolf Hitler exercised direct control over all German military operations. He determined the military strategy on all fronts and closely supervised the formulation of plans and their execution. Hitler did not trust the senior staff of the German Army. He therefore made many military decisions based on his own intuition and very limited military experience. Many senior Allied military and political leaders tended to feel that Hitler's interference with the operations of the German Army tended to help the Allied cause, rather than hinder it. *Real War Photos*

In this late war photo, Patton is seen surrounded by the principal staff officers of the Third Army. Seated at Patton's left is Brigadier General (later Major General) Hobart R. Gay, who replaced Major General Hugh J. Gaffey in December 1944 as Patton's Chief of Staff. As the original general staff officers of the Third Army arrived in England in early 1944, Patton quickly replaced them with members of his former Seventh Army command. Almost all of Patton's senior staff officers were former cavalrymen who shared an interest in armored warfare.
Patton Museum

Third Army. He knew the important battles for France and the path to Germany lay eastward in the direction of Paris, not westward in the opposite direction. It would take a few more days before Bradley would begin to see that Patton's opinion about the Brittany campaign was correct. Before the invasion of France, Allied planners believed it would take the entire Third Army to capture Brittany and its ports. Evidence of German disorganization in early August, however, convinced Allied leaders that the opportunity existed for seizing Brittany and its ports with much smaller forces.

On August 2, Bradley issued new orders for Patton that stated Brittany and its ports were to be seized using "only minimum force." Patton was well aware of the dire situation facing the Wehrmacht (German Army) in Brittany. He decided to clear Brittany with only his VIII Corps under the command of Middleton. Out of the forces available to the VIII Corps, three armored spearheads appeared. They would enter into battle with little or no infantry support. The two main armored spearheads used for the purpose of securing Brittany consisted of the hard-charging 4th and 6th Armored Divisions, which spent most of the northwestern European Campaign attached to Patton's Third Army.

A third armored spearhead sent into Brittany by VIII Corps consisted of a temporary unit called Task Force A with a strength of

The motto of the Tank Destroyer (TD) Branch was "Seek, Strike, Destroy." Patton had questioned the entire concept of TD at a very early stage in its development. Despite his lack of enthusiasm, and that of other senior officers, the army put ashore in France 19 self-propelled and 11 towed battalions of TDs. The main armament for the towed TDs battalions in France was the 3-inch gun M-5 shown here. By the end of the war most of the towed TD battalions were converted to self-propelled TD battalions.
National Archives

The American M-10 Tank Destroyer (TD) first saw action in North Africa in early 1943. Based on the lightened chassis of an M-4A2 Sherman medium tank, the M-10 weighed roughly 30 tons. Combat experience showed the M-10's 3-inch gun was unable to punch holes in late-war German tanks like the Panther or Tiger. In the British Army the American-supplied M-10s were rearmed with the high-velocity 17-pounder gun. *Patton Museum*

about 3,500 men. It consisted of a mixture of tank destroyer units, engineer units, and mechanized cavalry groups. The job of Task Force A was to protect a series of several bridges that carried a railroad line that generally ran along the north shore of Brittany. The railroad connected the Breton port of Brest to Rennes, and then ran into the interior of France. If the port at Brest fell intact into Third Army hands, the railroad would be a quick means of moving military supplies into France in support of all American military forces. Task Force A would also assist the VIII Corps in the capture of the ports of Saint Malo and Brest.

The Fourth Armored Division in Brittany

Major General John Shirley Wood, the commander of the Fourth Armored Division, was best known among his men as "Tiger Jack." Liddell Hart, the famous British military historian described Wood as: "The Rommel of the American armored forces . . . one of the most

One of the most remarkable American generals of the war in Europe, but virtually unknown to most Americans, was Major General John Shirley Wood, nicknamed "Tiger Jack." Wood was the aggressive commander of the "elite" Fourth Armored Division in Europe. Before his division began shipping out to England in early 1944, Wood informed his troops, "This division will attack and attack, and if an order is given to fall back, that order will not come from me." *Patton Museum*

Major General John Shirley Wood normally commanded his 4th Armored Division from the front, using a light liaison plane. Orders from corps headquarters were passed directly to his far-flung, fast-moving armored columns. Wood justified his frequent and prolonged absences from his division headquarters by saying, "If you can't see it happen, it's too late to hear about it back in a rear area and meet it with proper force." Pictured is an American M-4 Sherman tank firing at German positions on the opposite side of a French farmer's field. *National Archives*

dynamic commanders of armor in World War II and the first in the Allied Armies to demonstrate in Europe the essence of the art and tempo of handling a mobile force."

Despite the very strong protests of Wood, the 4th Armored Division received the job of driving southwest 40 miles from Pontaubault to capture the city of Rennes, the capital of the province of Brittany and an important road and communications center. Once the division captured Rennes, it was to continue its advance and seize the Quiberon Bay area 60 miles southwest of Rennes. In so doing, the 4th would cut off the Brittany peninsula near its base and prevent the reinforcement or escape of German forces within Brittany. There were also plans in the works to build a brand-new harbor in the Quiberon Bay area if the VIII Corps failed to capture undamaged any of the existing Breton ports.

Wood rightly saw the movement westward of his division as a waste of valuable time. Like Patton, he knew the real campaign for Europe lay eastward in the direction of Germany and not westward to the ocean. Unfortunately for Wood, the plans for seizing Brittany had been drawn up long before the invasion of France. Due to a great deal of strategic inflexibility among American senior commanders, the plans for the Brittany campaign were being doggedly carried out despite growing opportunities being created elsewhere. Eventually, the senior American commanders would see the error of their ways and prove Wood correct.

Most of the American armored divisions that saw action in Europe were organized into two groupings known as combat commands (CC), and a third known as the reserve command (CCR). These groupings were organized to provide a tactical headquarters for any mission a division commander might designate. Pictured in France is a first aid jeep, passing a column of M-4 Sherman tanks. The vegetation covering the tanks is to hide the vehicles from enemy artillery observers. *Real War Photos*

Elements of the 4th Armored Division reached the outskirts of Rennes on the morning of August 2. Strong German resistance, consisting of 88-mm antiaircraft guns supported by infantry with portable antitank rockets, managed to halt the advance of Wood's tank column.

Wood sent his tanks around the western side of the city and cut all lines of German communication from the west and south. At this point, he tried to turn his tanks in a southeastern direction but was overruled by the VIII Corps commander. The corps commander then informed Wood that he must not merely cut off Rennes but capture the city as well. To accomplish this added task, Wood brought up the 13th Infantry Regiment riding in trucks and a supporting artillery unit. He sent the Second Cavalry Group circling to the east of Rennes to prevent a German escape in that direction. Rennes finally fell to the 4th Armored Division on August 4. Despite the best efforts of Wood's troops, most of the 2,000 German troops defending the city managed to escape.

At the same time Rennes was surrounded, other elements of the division continued driving deeper into Brittany. On the afternoon of August 3, Wood's tanks captured the small towns of Bain-de-Bretagne and Derval, 30 and 40 miles south of Rennes. These armored elements of the 4th Armored Division represented

Any number of battalions could be attached to an armored division's Combat Command (CC), depending on its particular task. Each CC could be further divided into two or four smaller task forces. Additional units such as engineer, reconnaissance, and maintenance could also be added to each CC or task force. Pictured is an American tanker looking over the damage done to his M-4A3 Sherman tank (armed with a 76-mm gun) by a German anti-tank mine. *National Archives*

a very effective blocking force at the base of the Brittany peninsula.

With the capture of Rennes, the next major objective of the 4th Armored Division became the port city of Lorient. Before advancing on Lorient, Wood ordered that the small port of Vannes along the Quiberon Bay area be seized. Vannes sat along a main road and railway that led to Lorient. With the help of a local French Resistance unit, the town fell into American hands on August 5. It took place so quickly that the German defenders were unable to destroy any of the port's facilities, including bridges and railroads. With the capture of Vannes, Wood's 4th Armor Division had effectively cut the Brittany peninsula at its base.

Unlike the capture of Vannes, the capture of Lorient proved a much harder process for the

Pictured together in France are Patton and Major General Hugh J. Gaffey. Gaffey had served with Patton in different roles in the United States, North Africa, and Sicily. When Patton received command of the Third Army, he made Gaffey his Chief of Staff. Gaffey was originally an artilleryman who transferred to the armor branch before America entered World War II. He was considered both an excellent staff officer and a tank expert. In Sicily, Gaffey commanded the Second Armored Division. *Patton Museum*

4th Armored Division. The Germans, numbering almost 11,000 troops as well as having a large submarine base at Lorient, put up a stiff fight. Advanced elements of the 4th Division reaching the city on August 7 found strong defenses that included antitank ditches and minefields covered by antitank guns and artillery. The division probed the city's defenses and concluded that it could not take the port with its existing strength. On August 8, Middleton told Wood, "Do not become involved in a fight for Lorient unless [the] enemy attacks." Wood was to seal off the port until relieved by other units. This wouldn't happen until August 15, when the last element of the 4th Armored Division was finally relieved of guarding Lorient.

On August 10, Wood received orders from Middleton to capture the port of Nantes, located 88 miles east of Lorient. Elements of the Fourth Armored Division reached the outskirts of Nantes on August 11. With the help of the local French Resistance, the division captured the port on August 12. Unfortunately for the Allies, the Germans managed to destroy the port's facilities before their capture.

During the first 12 days of August, the fast-moving and aggressive 4th Armored Division captured almost 5,000 German prisoners and destroyed or captured almost 250 German vehicles. During this same period the division lost 98 killed, 362 wounded, and 11 missing. In addition, the division lost only 15 combat vehicles and 20 other vehicles.

The Sixth Armored Division in Brittany

The 6th Armored Division was commanded by Major General Robert W. Grow. Like Patton, Grow was a long-time cavalryman who took up the cause of armored warfare in the 1930s. Patton described Grow as, "one of the best armored forces commanders the war produced."

The advance of Grow's division into Brittany began on the morning of August 1. The original goal, as set by Middleton, was the small Brittany town of Dinan, located west of Pontaubault. A couple of hours after Grow's division had received its marching orders from Middleton, Patton showed up and told Grow he wanted his division to capture the large and important deep-water port of Brest within five days. Brest sat at the western tip of the Brittany peninsula and was over 200 miles away from the division's location. In order to speed its

Besides its tank battalions, every American armored division had three field artillery battalions. Each battalion was further divided into three firing batteries. Most battalions were equipped with the M-7 self-propelled 105-mm howitzer. The howitzer was mounted in the right front of a boxlike open-top hull of a specially modified M-3 or M-4 tank chassis. For antiaircraft protection the M-7 carried a .50-caliber M-2 machine gun in an antiaircraft mount located next to the 105-mm howitzer. Shown here is the crew of an M-7 cleaning the barrel of its 105-mm howitzer. *National Archives*

For additional artillery support, American armored divisions often had a battalion of M-12 self-propelled 155-mm guns attached. The 155-mm guns (M-4) dated from World War I, and were mounted on specially modified chassis of obsolete M-3 medium tanks. During the advance of Patton's armored division in France, the M-12s were often the only heavy artillery available for fire support missions. *National Archives*

advance, Patton told Grow to bypass any German resistance. In quick order, Grow stopped the advance on Dinan and began trying to reorganize his division into two parallel columns for the drive to Brest. As Middleton became

Mechanized cavalry groups were the major ground reconnaissance units of the American Army. They were lightly armored and performed reconnaissance missions in small teams of armored cars and jeeps. In March 1944, Patton issued a set of written guidelines to his troops in which he discussed his belief in the value of reconnaissance, "You can never have too much reconnaissance. Use every means available before, during, and after battle. Reports must be facts, not opinions; negative as well as positive." A lack of good reconnaissance could result in heavy losses to American forces. Pictured are American soldiers firing at German positions with their jeep-mounted .50-caliber M-2 machine gun. American factories built almost 640,000 jeeps during the war years. *National Archives*

A mechanized cavalry group consisted of a group headquarters and headquarters troop. The troop consisted of two mechanized cavalry reconnaissance squadrons. Each reconnaissance squadron normally had six jeeps and six armored cars, crewed by 2 officers and 28 enlisted men. Wartime reconnaissance units employed the six-wheeled M-8 armored car pictured here. The M-8 had a four-man crew and was armed with a turret-mounted 37-mm gun and two machine guns. *National Archives*

aware of the change in plan, he attached additional units, including a battalion of self-propelled 155-mm guns and an antiaircraft unit, to the 6th Armored Division.

Despite some initial German resistance on August 1, the 6th Armored found clear going in Brittany on the morning of August 2 and advanced nearly 35 miles. That evening, Grow had to stop so his men could get some badly needed rest. He decided that his division would continue its advance to Brest the next day. This pause allowed Grow to place his mechanized cavalry squadrons at the front and on the flanks of the two armored columns.

The 6th Armored Division resumed its advance on Brest as scheduled. Meeting only minor German resistance, the division managed to push another 30 miles deeper into Brittany. To everyone's surprise, Middleton called a halt to the advance that same afternoon. He had decided he needed the 6th Armored Division to assist Task Force A and the 83rd Infantry Division in capturing the town of Dinan and the port city of Saint Malo. The port lay 50 miles west of Avranches and was an important pre-invasion objective assigned to the Third Army. Patton considered the capture of Saint Malo incidental to the entire Brittany campaign. Middleton was much more cautious than Patton, believing the capture of Saint Malo had to happen before the advance to Brest could take place.

As the disappointed staff officers of the 6th Armored Division began making plans to attack Dinan, Patton arrived at the division's headquarters. He was unaware that Middleton had changed the division's orders. When Patton came face to face with Grow, he angrily asked, "What in hell are you doing sitting here? I

Thirteen mechanized cavalry groups and one unattached cavalry reconnaissance squadron fought in Europe during World War II. Groups were assigned to armies, and typically attached to corps. Most of these attachments were permanent. Corps frequently attached these units, for operations only, to infantry divisions. Pictured on a reconnaissance mission is an M-8 armored car followed by three jeeps. The crew of the armored car has added a welded metal basket to the front of its vehicle. It contains sandbags for added protection from German weapons. *National Archives*

In the performance of offensive, defensive, and security missions, it was normal for the mechanized cavalry groups to be reinforced by a battalion of field artillery, a company of combat engineers, and a battalion of tank destroyers. Pictured somewhere in France, guarding a street corner, is an M-18 tank destroyer (TD). It was armed with a 76-mm gun and a single .50-caliber machine gun, seen in the picture, mounted on a tripod in front of the vehicle. *National Archives*

Besides the mechanized cavalry groups attached to armies, there also existed more than 100 divisional cavalry units, including an armored reconnaissance battalion that formed part of the Second and Third Armored Divisions. Each infantry division had a reconnaissance troop of 155 men as a normal attachment. Combat experience showed that cavalry units rarely performed pure reconnaissance missions. Their most common tasks were defensive in nature. Pictured is an M-20 armored utility car, basically a turretless M-8 armored car armed with a .50-caliber machine gun. *National Archives*

All American tank battalions that served in northwest Europe after D-Day contained one company of light tanks. The role of these tanks was to provide a fast, highly mobile element for reconnaissance and to act as a covering force for the medium tanks of the battalion. The standard American light tank employed in 1944 was the M-5A1, pictured here. It weighed 15 tons, had a four-man crew, and was armed with a 37-mm gun and three .30-caliber machine guns. *Patton Museum*

Patton's fast-moving armored columns depended primarily on radio communications to stay in touch with their higher headquarters. Sadly, the radio equipment provided by the Signal Corps proved unequal to the task. Communications soon broke down completely in Brittany. The VIII Corps commander often had little or no contact with the 4th and 6th Armored Divisions as they raced through Brittany. Pictured is an M-4 Sherman tank that had driven off a road and overturned *National Archives*

thought I told you to go to Brest." Grow explained to Patton that his advance to Brest had been halted. "On what authority?" Patton rasped. "Corps order, sir," Grow said as he handed to Patton the actual written message received from Middleton halting his advance to Brest. Patton read the note and told Grow, "I'll see Middleton. You go ahead where I told you to go."

Grow assured Patton that his division could quickly continue the advance to Brest. Patton admitted to Grow that he was surprised to have found his division so far into Brittany. An aide who had accompanied Patton later told Grow that Patton had to throw away several maps during the trip to the division command post. Each time he ran off one map onto another was an occasion for jubilant profanity.

Restarting the 6th Armored Division toward Brest proved harder than Grow had hoped. The division ran into blown bridges and heavily mined crossing points on the evening of August 4. He decided to take advantage of a full moon and clear weather to order a night march. Local French Resistance groups acted as guides to Grow's armored columns. Avoiding German strong points, the 6th Armored managed to reach the town of Huelgoat, less than 40 miles from Brest, on the morning of August 5. Hope arose that the division could be in Brest by nightfall, thereby meeting Patton's deadline. Unfortunately for Grow, a force of 500 Germans armed with artillery and tanks near Huelgoat took several hours to clear. Unwilling to advance on Brest in darkness, Grow planned to launch his tanks at Brest on the morning of August 6. One of the two armored columns got within 15 miles of Brest on the evening of August 6. At that point, heavy German opposition abruptly halted the American advance.

Grow remained convinced that he could take Brest by August 7 in a surprise attack. His tanks did get to within seven miles north of the port on August 7 before running into strong German defensive positions and heavy artillery fire. From that point on, it became clear the Germans would not give up Brest without a strong fight. Grow tried to bluff the German commander of Brest into surrendering on August 8, but the Germans rejected the offer.

The 6th Armored Division had little hard information on the strength of the German defenses around Brest. The best guess of the division's staff estimated the defenders in Brest numbered no more than 3,000 men. In reality,

As an army commander, Patton always wanted to know where his units were. In order to accomplish this goal Patton renamed the 6th Mechanized Cavalry Group, attached to the Third Army, as the "Army Information Service" and changed it into a communications unit. The renamed unit soon gained the nickname of "Patton's Household Cavalry." Patton's Household Cavalry normally attached a single M-8 armored car with a high-powered radio, as well as several armored jeeps, to each armored division. The radio in the M-8 armored car provided a direct radio link to Patton's headquarters. The armored jeeps carried written reports to Patton's headquarters when radios failed. Here, an American Army jeep armed with a .50-caliber machine gun is passing a German soldier who died defending France for Hitler. *National Archives*

the German defenders numbered close to 38,000 army, navy, and air force troops by the time Grow launched his first attacks on Brest on August 11 and 12. Outnumbered and outgunned, the Sixth Armored Division made little progress against the German defensive positions.

During the battle for the port of Saint Malo, American infantrymen became involved in fierce street fighting with the German defenders. Pictured here is an American officer looking at a German soldier who killed three of the officer's men before he himself was killed. The last German position defending Saint Malo did not surrender until September 2. In its efforts to capture the city, the Americans had to destroy it beyond repair. *National Archives*

Sensing the difficulty in capturing Brest with his existing forces, Grow requested that Middleton send infantry, heavy artillery, and engineer units to his aid. Unfortunately again for Grow, most of the supporting units he needed from the VIII Corps remained engaged in trying to capture the port of Saint Malo. On the evening of August 12, Grow received orders to contain Brest with one element of his division and send the rest to Lorient and Vannes to relieve the 4th Armored Division. Grow completed the relief at Lorient and Vannes on August 14.

In the advance to Brest, the hard-charging 6th Armored Division captured more than 4,000 German prisoners and destroyed a number of German vehicles. In exchange, the division lost 130 men killed, about 400 wounded, and 70 missing. The division also lost 50 combat vehicles and 62 other assorted vehicles during the advance.

After the capture of Saint Malo, most of the VIII Corps moved to capture Brest on August 25. Despite an impressive amount of Allied sup-

American artillerymen in Brittany prepare to fire their 105-mm M-3 howitzer at the German defenders of Brest. The M-3 was originally designated as an infantry field gun, and later issued to airborne artillery units. It consisted of a cut-down 105-mm howitzer barrel mounted on a modified 75-mm gun carriage. It was lighter and more maneuverable than the standard M-2 105-mm howitzer. Due to its lighter weight and length, it did not have the range or hitting power of its larger cousin. *National Archives*

port from the air, Brest did not surrender until September 20. By the time of its capture, the port facilities had suffered so much damage they were beyond any hope of immediate repair. It took almost 50,000 troops to subdue the approximately 75 German strong points that had made up Brest's defenses. American casualties totaled almost 10,000 men.

Why the American Army devoted so much time and effort in trying to capture a port that they knew the Germans would destroy before it was allowed to fall into their hands remains unclear. Many historians and writers point out that the men and equipment involved in trying to capture Brest in September 1944 would have been much more useful in Patton's eastward advance. At the time, Bradley told Patton that it was important to the prestige of the American Army to not lose a battle and therefore Brest had to fall at all costs. Patton later wrote: "We both [Bradley and Patton] felt that the taking of Brest at that time was useless, because it was too far away and the harbor was badly destroyed. On the other hand, we agreed that, when the

Among the larger artillery pieces employed by the American Army to subdue the German defenders of Brest was the 240-mm howitzer M-1, pictured here at the moment of firing. The VIII Corps commander used 15 medium and heavy battalions of corps artillery against Brest. In the end, it took the combined actions by heavy artillery fire (more than 200,000 rounds), infantry assaults, engineer blasting operations, and the use of flamethrowers before Brest surrendered on September 18. *National Archives*

Before Brest fell into American hands, the German defenders thoroughly demolished the port, as can be clearly seen in this photo. This included bridges, wharves, dry docks, cranes along the waterfront, even the breakwaters enclosing the naval basin and the commercial port. The Germans also scuttled ships in the harbor area. The American campaign to capture Brest had also contributed to the overall destruction of a once-thriving port. *National Archives*

line up to go into action. The first of Patton's other corps to go into action was Major General Wade H. Haislip's XV Corps. Like many other American generals at the time, Haislip had fought in France during World War I.

The XV Corps arrived in Normandy in mid-July. In the original invasion plans, the XV Corps would have assisted VIII Corps in the overrunning of Brittany. As it became clear to American military leaders that only a single corps needed to be in Brittany, the deployment of the XV Corps remained uncertain. Even the question of what divisions were going to become part of the corps remained up in the air. At the last moment, the corps received the 5th Armored Division and the 83rd and 90th Infantry Divisions. The 5th Armored Division, commanded by Major General Lunsford E. Oliver, had just arrived in Normandy, while the

As Patton's VIII Corps overran Brittany with the 4th and 6th Armored Divisions, the other corps of his Third Army joined the battle. The first to enter action, after the VIII Corps, was the XV Corps under the command of Major General Wade H. Haislip (pictured). Like Patton, Haislip was a West Pointer who had fought in France in World War I. The job assigned to the divisions of the XV Corps was to protect the Avranches corridor through which all the Third Army had to pass to enter Brittany and beyond. *National Archives*

In the rear areas the army was forced to depend on telephone lines to cope with the heavy volume of communication traffic between all the various units. In the four months following the landing in France, the Allies laid over 100,000 circuit miles of telephone line. Patton once wrote, "Push wire communications to the limit. A wire phone is worth three radios for both speed and security." Somewhere in France, an Army Signal Corps technician is shown checking phone lines. *National Archives*

American Army had once put its hands to the plow, it should not let go. Therefore, it was necessary to take Brest." Many others suggest that the battle for Brest had more to do with the strategic inflexibility of both Eisenhower and Bradley in pursuing the pre-invasion plans despite ever-changing circumstances.

The Rest of Third Army Comes on Line

Even as the armored divisions of VIII Corps plunged deeper into Brittany, the remaining three corps of Patton's Third Army began to

Pictured is a heavily camouflaged M-10 tank destroyer (TD), that has just destroyed an unarmored German half-track (prime mover) seen in the background. Crews spoke highly of the M-10, despite its firepower disadvantage versus German tanks. They especially admired the M-10 for its versatility and for the reliability of its twin diesel engines. Instead of hunting down German tanks, as they were originally designed for, the primary task of the TDs became infantry support.
National Archives

infantry divisions came from the First Army. All three divisions went into action an hour before midnight on August 1.

The initial combat goal of the XV Corps was to establish a large protective barrier around the narrow Avranches bottleneck. If the Germans decided to counterattack the Third Army breakout, Avranches would be the logical target. By capturing Avranches, German forces could cut off the VIII Corps' supply lines. To prevent this, the XV Corps advanced in a southeastern direction 15 miles out of Avranches to the town of Saint Hilaire-du-Harcouët where it took up a position between the VIII Corps and the First Army's VII Corps on August 2. To further secure the Third Army's flank, the 106th Mechanized Cavalry Group captured the town of Fougeres on August 3.

The German forces opposite the First Army continued to fight with a determined tenacity. In contrast, the German forces facing the Third Army continued to fall apart. A large gap appeared in front of the XV Corps. Patton, as

well as the other Allied military leaders, began to see a golden opportunity for an eastward breakout into central France. This new interest in a quick eastward advance differed sharply from the Allied preinvasion plans. In those plans the Allies had not even considered an eastward advance into central France until the Brittany ports were in American hands. With new opportunities presenting themselves, the significance attached to seizing the Breton ports steadily diminished throughout the month of August.

Patton set up the Third Army headquarters in Beauchamps, 11 miles north of Avranches, on August 2. The Luftwaffe managed to bomb the headquarters on the night of August 6, but caused no casualties. At the time, the news blackout ordered by Eisenhower on the arrival of the Third Army in France was still in effect. It was finally lifted on August 15, during a press conference given by Eisenhower. By that time, the Germans were well aware of Patton's arrival.

The knowledge that Patton was in France

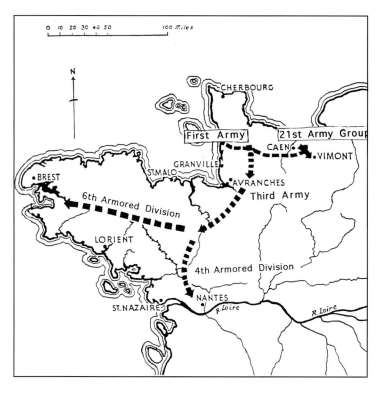

This map shows the advance of Patton's Third Army's armored divisions through Brittany in July 1944. The German-held port of Brest did not fall into American hands until September 20, 1944. The German-held ports of Lorient and Saint Nazaire held out until the official German surrender in May 1945. The Loire River would act as the southern flank of Patton's Third Army through much of his early campaign in France. *U.S. Army map*

The next corps to enter battle as part of Patton's Third Army was the XX Corps under the command of Lieutenant General Walton H. Walker. Besides two American infantry divisions, the XX Corps also contained the Free French 2nd Armored Division. Pictured in a Normandy assembly area is a tank battalion of the French armored division. The American Army trained and equipped five French infantry divisions in addition to the Free French 2nd Armored Division. *National Archives*

and in charge of the Third Army was actually a relief to Hitler and the German High Command. No longer would they fear a second Allied invasion landing in Pas de Calais. Despite the release of additional German military man-

power from the Fifteenth Army, it was too late for these German troops to change the outcome of the war. The effectiveness of Patton and his mythical First Army Group in tying down German troops during the crucial battle for Normandy had far exceeded anyone's hopes.

Patton's XX Corps in Action

The Allied leaders formulated plans for an eastward advance toward Paris. At the same time, Patton's Third Army received some new assignments that included securing a 60-mile stretch of terrain and bridges along the Mayenne River that oriented along a north/south axis. Patton also had to protect his right flank along the Loire River, which oriented along an east/west axis. To complete these assignments Patton brought the XX Corps commanded by Lieutenant General Walton H. Walker into line on August 6. The corps originally consisted of the 5th and 35th Infantry Divisions plus the Free French 2nd Armored Division, commanded by Major General Jacques Philippe Leclerc, which the Americans had helped organize, equip, and train.

Patton had received a strong warning from his senior intelligence officer that there were enough German forces on the other side of the Loire River to mount a serious counterattack. Walker's XX Corps did not have sufficient forces to adequately guard the entire Loire River flank. Patton therefore decided to use the pilots and planes of the XIX TAC to guard the Loire River flank. XIX TAC planes accomplished the job by flying armed reconnaissance missions south of the Loire River throughout the month of August. No threat of a German counterattack ever appeared along the Loire River flank during August. Patton would later describe the relationship between XIX TAC and his Third Army as "love at first sight."

The XV Corps began its advance on the Mayenne River 30 miles from Saint Hilaire-du-Harcouët on August 5. The river itself was a serious obstacle about 100 feet wide and 5 feet deep. All the bridges except one at the town of Mayenne were in ruins. If the bridge over the Mayenne River fell intact to the XV Corps, it could move on to capture the town of Laval. The loss of Laval would be a serious blow to the Germans since it would threaten Le Mans and Alencon, both important German communications and supply centers. Knowing that the fighting during the next few days might be decisive for the entire western European campaign, Haislip urged his commanders "to push all personnel to the limits of human endurance."

Elements of the fast-moving XV Corps reached the Mayenne River by noon on August 5. They found the bridge intact. Brushing aside minor German resistance, the American troops quickly captured both the bridge and town. Other elements of the XV Corps also reached the Mayenne River on August 5, crossing it on bridges built by engineers. On August 6, elements of the XV Corps captured Laval. Even before the town's capture, Patton received per-

A German defender in Brittany unlucky enough to find himself in the path of Patton's 4th or 6th Armored Divisions first had to deal with the fighter-bombers of the XIX Tactical Air Command (TAC). The pilots and planes of TAC maintained constant patrols in advance of Patton's armored divisions. Army Air Force liaison officers riding in lead tanks called out targets for the fighter-bombers, and kept the ground troops informed as to what lay ahead of the column. The standard fighter-bomber of TAC was the P-47 Thunderbolt, seen here with invasion markings. *Real War Photos*

The last of Patton's corps to enter into battle was the XII Corps, commanded by Major General Manton S. Eddy, pictured here to Patton's left. On Patton's right is Major General Horace L. MacBride, commander of the 80th Infantry Division of Patton's Third Army. Eddy arrived in Normandy as commander of the 9th Infantry Division. He was given command of the XII Corps when the original commander (Major General R. Cook) had to be relieved due to health problems on August 19. *Patton Museum*

In order to drive a wedge between the American First and Third Armies in Normandy and Brittany, Hitler ordered a large armored counterattack aimed at Avranches on August 6. Hitler had high hopes that the offensive could throw the Allies back to the sea. The German field commanders assigned to the mission were a lot less optimistic about its chances of success. The counterattack began shortly after midnight on August 7. Due to the great haste in which the German counterattack had been planned, not all of the German units designated for the operation reached their assembly areas in time. Instead of a well-massed, coordinated effort, only two of the three panzer divisions set to lead the assault jumped off on time. Despite these problems the German attackers achieved some initial success by capturing Mortain under the cover of darkness. Shown here is a squad of German panzer grenadiers, onboard their armored half-track, cautiously looking for any sign of Allied troops or tanks. *Patton Museum*

mission from Bradley to send the XV Corps on to Le Mans. To reach it, the corps would have to pass through 45 miles of highly defensible terrain and cross a major river. Without missing a beat, the XV Corps captured Le Mans on August 8, with only very light casualties. In the four days it took Patton's XV Corps to advance the 75 miles from Saint Hilaire-du-Harcouët to Le Mans, it had captured over 7,000 enemy prisoners. It had also frustrated German plans to organize strong defensive positions at both Laval and Le Mans.

On August 12, Patton brought the last of the Third Army's four corps into line: the XII Corps commanded by Major General Gilbert R.

Cook. Due to reasons of Cook's health, Patton replaced him with Major General Manton S. Eddy seven days later. Patton attached the Fourth Armored Division and the 35th Infantry Division to the newly arrived corps, and assigned it the job of protecting the Third Army's southern flank.

The German Counterattack

The 12th Army Group staff officers began planning the next advance. Bradley knew from the Magic/Ultra reports that the Germans were planning a counterattack aimed at Avranches. In the early morning hours of August 7, the commander of the German Seventh Army launched the counterattack to regain Avranches and to reestablish German defensive lines in Normandy. Hitler saw it as a last chance to throw the Allies back toward the sea. Unfortunately for Hitler, none of his field commanders shared his conviction. Most felt the counterattack was doomed to failure before it began.

The German counterattack consisted of four underpowered armored divisions with a total of about 150 tanks. They included the Army 2nd and 116th Panzer Divisions, and the 1st and 2nd Waffen SS Panzer Divisions. One of their most important targets was the small town of Mortain. If Mortain fell into German hands, they could then sweep westward on to Avranches, roughly 10 miles away. In the official Army history, the German counterattack became known as the "Mortain Counterattack." Ever fearful of Allied air superiority, the Luftwaffe had promised to furnish hundreds of planes to protect the advancing German armored columns.

In the darkness, the Second Waffen SS Panzer Division, advancing in two columns, captured the town of Mortain. As the division continued its advance, one column neared the high ground west of the town and then westward toward Saint Hilaire-du-Harcouët. If they could capture Saint Hilaire-du-Harcouët, they would be less than four miles from Avranches. Before the German tanks could reach their goal, they had to deal with a battalion (roughly 700 men) of the 30th Infantry Division, which had deployed its troops on a high hill (Hill 317) east of Mortain. From Hill 317 the American soldiers had a commanding view of the area around Mortain. They used this advantage to call in artillery fire, causing heavy casualties among the advancing German tankers. Despite repeated German attacks, the cutoff and surrounded American troops of the Second Battalion held on to their position until finally relieved on August 12.

Other German armored columns also ran into heavy American resistance that brought their advance to a halt. By the morning of August 7, the German armored columns managed to penetrate about six miles into the First Army lines. When Allied planes arrived over the enemy armored columns in the early morning

As the sun rose on the morning of August 7, the fog that the Germans had hoped would hide them from Allied fighter-bombers failed to appear. The German tankers quickly sought cover for their vehicles from the expected aerial attack. Before the Allied fighter-bombers arrived on the scene, American artillery delivered a murderous hail of fire on the German armored columns. The artillery was soon joined by Allied planes that added to the rain of destruction. Pictured is a burned-out German Panther tank (model A) that had sought cover from Allied planes by trying to hide inside a hedgerow. *Patton Museum*

American artillery played an important role in stopping the German offensive. A German intelligence bulletin described American artillery, "It is adaptable and is skilled at concentrated precision fire delivered by large formations." Pictured is a destroyed German 12-ton prime mover (half-track) caught in an American artillery barrage. *National Archives*

The overwhelming air superiority of the Allies forced the Germans to move many of their units at night. To provide protection from air attacks during daylight hours, the Germans supplied their panzer divisions with the quadruple 2-cm (20-mm) Flakvierling 38 (antiaircraft gun), as seen in this picture. It was mounted on both half-tracks and fully tracked vehicles within the panzer divisions. It had an effective ceiling of 3,500 feet and could fire up to 700 to 800 rounds per minute. *National Archives*

hours of August 7, however, the tide of battle quickly turned. The Allied planes began a series of fierce bombing and strafing attacks that caused the Germans to abandon many of their tanks.

The air cover promised by the Luftwaffe never appeared. Allied planes had effectively engaged or destroyed every supporting German plane. By the morning of August 8, the First Army estimated the German forces involved in the Mortain Counterattack had fewer than 25 tanks remaining. The German commander of the Seventh Army could see the handwriting on the wall and ordered a halt to the offensive attack shortly before midnight on August 8.

Patton, like Bradley, had received advance warning of the German counterattack through Ultra. Prior to this moment, Patton had little interest in or knowledge of the information that Ultra could provide about German military intentions. After the counterattack, Patton insisted on an Ultra briefing every morning. Despite the advance warning about a possible German counterattack, Patton originally believed the German effort was only a ruse designed to cover a withdrawal.

As the size of the German counterattack became more apparent to Patton, he quickly realized that it could pose a threat to the narrow Avranches corridor through which all the Third Army supplies flowed. He directed Major Gen-

Allied fighter-bombers took an ever-increasing toll on the German armored columns heading toward Avranches on August 7. The German commander in overall control of the counterattack decided the attack had failed and requested permission from Hitler to withdraw his forces. Hitler would have none of that, and decided to take a more direct role in the operation. Pictured is a turretless Sturmgeschutz IV, armed with a high-velocity 75-mm gun, destroyed by Allied aircraft. *Real War Photos*

eral Walker's XX Corps to divert part of his corps from its planned move south, and rush it to the threatened area to assist the First Army in halting the German counterattack. At this time, the XX Corps was already on the move with the Fifth Infantry Division located some eight miles south of Vitre, and the remainder of the corps was near Saint Hilaire-au-Harcouët. Walker immediately decided to use those elements nearest the threat, the 35th Infantry Division. At the same time, the 2nd Free French

Armored Division was ordered to send a task force to guard the bridge at Saint Hilaire-du-Harcouët. As the 35th Infantry Division moved northward to help stop the German counterattack, a part of the XX Corps Headquarters was moving southward to Vitre to establish an advanced command post.

Upon arriving in Vitre, General Gaffey, Chief of Staff of Patton's Third Army, informed the XX Corps headquarters of the developments and of their general's decision to use the

Despite the many problems besieging the German counterattack aimed at Avranches, the loss of Mortain was a serious blow to the First Army. From the North of Mortain, German forces threatened the rear areas of the VII Corps. It fell to the men of the 30th Infantry Division to recapture Mortain. After a series of bloody, small-unit battles, the Germans withdrew from Mortain on August 11, leaving almost 100 tanks in the area. Pictured is a German Jagdpanzer IV (turretless tank destroyer) that took a high-velocity round in its lower front hulls.
Patton Museum

forces remaining in the vicinity of Saint Hilaire-du-Harcouët. Gaffey also directed that the corps attack to the south toward Angers and Nantes with the 5th Infantry Division now at Vitre. The XX Corps captured Angers on August 10, thus effectively guarding the southern flank of the XV Corps' advances.

Walker now had two important jobs. The first was to protect the Avranches corridor against the German counterattack, now in full force; the second was to continue the drive to the south. Thus, during its first major action, the XX Corps was creating military history by fighting on two fronts separated by some 75 miles. The First Army recaptured Mortain from the Germans on August 12. The retreating German armored divisions left more than 100 of their destroyed and abandoned tanks in the area around Mortain at the close of the battle.

Bradley was so confident in his ability to contain the German advance toward Avranches that he wrote on August 8 that the Mortain counterattack "had apparently been contained." As he studied his maps, Bradley quickly concluded that the Germans had made a serious tactical mistake. By sending the mass of their armored forces into the area southwest of

Falaise, they had given the British and American armies an opportunity to trap them between the towns of Falaise and Argentan, the "Falaise Gap."

Bradley knew if he could successfully close this gap the 150,000 men of the German Seventh Army and Fifth Panzer Army (formerly known as Panzer Group West) would be trapped. With the approval of Eisenhower and Montgomery, he decided to change the planned eastward drive of Patton's Third Army into a northeastern advance to take advantage of the German blunder.

On August 9, Eisenhower wrote a letter to Chief of Staff of the Army and Chairman of the Joint Chiefs of Staff Committee General Marshall describing the change in plans. In the letter, he explained, "Patton has the marching wing which will turn in rather sharply to the northeast from the general vicinity of Le Mans and just to the west thereof marching toward Alencon and Falaise. The enemy's bitter resistance and counterattack in the area between Mortain and south of Caen makes it appear that we have a good chance to encircle and destroy a lot of his forces."

Chapter Four

PATTON'S ADVANCE CONTINUES

Prior to Patton launching his XV Corps in a northeastern direction to encircle the German Seventh and Fifth Panzer Army, the First Canadian Army located north of the Germans began a southward advance on August 8. The actual timing of the Canadian attack was accidental—it came about before the Germans launched their Mortain Counterattack.

The First Canadian Army under the command of Lieutenant General Henry D.G. Crerar came into existence on August 1. Half the army consisted of British troops, and included a Polish armored division. The Canadian advance consisted of 600 tanks heading from Caen toward Falaise. Falaise was 21 miles southeast of Caen. If the Canadians captured Falaise quickly, they could move on to seize Argentan. Canadian success in securing not only Falaise but Argentan would have made unnecessary the northeastern advance of the XV Corps.

Patton's forces reached their assigned goals far ahead of the Canadian First Army. Facing stiff German resistance, the Canadian tanks halted eight miles short of Falaise on August 9. They proved unable to restart their advance on to Falaise until August 14 and did not reach the town until the evening of August 16. When the Canadians finally secured Falaise, a 15-mile gap, which became known as the Falaise Gap or Falaise Pocket, still remained between them and Patton's troops located south of Argentan.

Patton's XV Corps had set off from Le Mans toward Alencon on August 10. To increase the striking power of the advance, Patton added the Free French 2nd Armored Division to the XV Corps. Patton ordered Haislip to lead his advance to Alencon with his two armored divisions. Alencon fell on August 12. With its capture, Patton's XV Corps had a clear shot at

An hour before midnight on August 7, the Canadian First Army launched a massive tank attack against German lines. The attack was referred to as "Operation Totalize." The goal of the operation was to capture the town of Falaise, which lay 21 miles south of the Canadian staging area near Caen. The Canadian ground assault was preceded by a massive aerial and artillery bombardment. Pictured is a Canadian M-4A4 Sherman command tank, as evidenced by the extra radio antenna on the front hull. *Patton Museum*

In the darkness of night, the Canadian attack made good progress. By the morning of August 8, the Canadians achieved all their initial objectives. From that point on, the Canadian attack quickly foundered against stiff German resistance. The German defenders consisted of two infantry divisions and a single panzer division, backed up by fifty 88-mm antiaircraft guns, set up for antitank action. Pictured is a Canadian M-4A4 Sherman tank, taking cover near a French church. *Patton Museum*

Lying in the center of a small French town is this German Panther tank (model G) destroyed by Canadian forces. The Canadians continued their attack until August 9, when it lost all its momentum, for a gain of only eight miles. To restart their thrust toward Falaise, the Canadians launched another attack named Operation Tractable on August 14. The town of Falaise finally fell to the Canadians on August 17. *Patton Museum*

As the Canadian First Army fought desperately to reach Falaise in the face of stiff German resistance, Patton's XV Corps, advancing northward, reached its objective, the town of Argentan, on August 12. Unlike the troops of the Canadian First Army, the American soldiers of the XV Corps met only light German resistance. From the area around Argentan, it was less than 15 miles to Falaise. Pictured are American soldiers entering the town of Argentan. *National Archives*

capturing the town of Argentan, which lay roughly 20 miles north of Alencon. At either Argentan or Falaise, the XV Corps could link up with the Canadian First Army and complete the encirclement of the German Seventh Army and the Fifth Panzer Army. Meanwhile, the British Second Army and U.S. First Army would continue attacking along the westward front of the German forces. On the night of August 12, the Fifth Armored Division managed to reach the outskirts of Argentan, an important transportation and supply center for the Germans.

Generalfeldmarschall Guenther von Kluge, the German Seventh Army commander, easily figured out what was happening. He frantically sought permission from Hitler's headquarters to make a short, sharp armored thrust at Patton's forces. Hitler only wanted to know if Kluge could continue his counterattack toward Avranches from Mortain. On the morning of August 11, Hitler received information that another strike at Avranches was no longer feasible. He also received an ultimatum from von

The original Allied plans called for Patton's XV Corps to advance northward from Argentan. At the same time, the Canadian First Army was to advance southward from Falaise, meeting the Americans somewhere in the middle of the so-called Falaise Gap. This would have resulted in cutting off the only escape route eastward toward the Seine River for the roughly 150,000 German soldiers of the Seventh and Fifth Panzer Armies located in the Falaise Pocket. Pictured is an antiaircraft battery of German 88-mm guns, captured by advancing American forces in France. *National Archives*

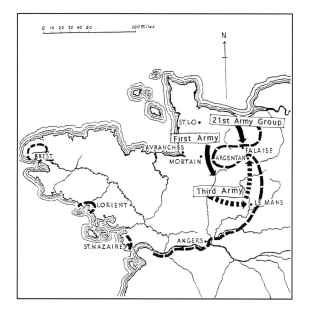

This map shows the movement of the Allied armies in August 1944 to close the area between the towns of Argentan and Falaise, referred to as the Falaise Gap. By closing the Falaise Gap, the Allied Armies could trap 150,000 German soldiers west of the gap in an area referred to as the Falaise Pocket. The northward advance of Patton's XV Corps was halted by Bradley on August 13, who feared it could be overrun by German forces retreating eastward through the Falaise Gap. *U.S. Army map*

Kluge stating that, unless a strong attack began immediately against Patton's advancing forces, his army would be cut off and unable to withdraw from its current positions. Hitler finally gave his approval for a counterattack against Patton's fast-advancing XV Corps on the evening of August 11. To assist in the counterattack, Hitler also granted permission for the Seventh Army to withdraw its forces eastward from Mortain. Despite their best efforts, the Germans could not muster enough men or equipment to conduct an attack large enough to stop the XV Corps.

On August 13, Kluge officially canceled the planned counterattack. The remaining German resources would try to maintain a defensive line against the advancing XV Corps. On the same day, General der Panzertruppen Josef "Sepp" Dietrich, the German commander of the Fifth Panzer Army, informed Hitler's headquarters, "If every effort is not made to move the forces toward the east and out of the threatened encirclement, the army group will have to write off both armies. Within a short time, resupplying the troops with ammunition and fuel will no longer be possible. Therefore, immediate measures are necessary to move to the east before such movement is definitely too late. It will soon be possible for the enemy to fire into the pocket with artillery from all sides."

On the morning of August 13, the 5th Armored Division tried to advance north to

From August 16 to August 21, the Canadian First Army's inability to reach Falaise at the same time Patton's XV Corps reached Argentan allowed the Germans to withdraw many of their troops through the gap between the two forces. Pictured here are American soldiers examining a captured German tank. The tank in this case is a World War I French Renault FT-17 light tank pressed into German service. Tanks of such vintage were employed by the Germans in police and airfield defense duties. *National Archives*

Falaise by driving around Argentan. It quickly ran into heavy German fire from the high ground north of the town and made no progress. That afternoon, a patrol from the Free French Second Armored Division managed to briefly enter Argentan before German tanks forced it to retreat. Exhausted, the German defenders braced themselves for the next attack, knowing they might be unable to stop Patton's tanks. To the utter surprise of the German troops, the Americans did not attack.

Unknown to the Germans, a surprising order from Bradley arrived at the XV Corps headquarters in the early afternoon stating that the XV Corps must stop its northward advance toward Falaise. It also ordered that any elements of the corps that might be "in the vicinity of Falaise or to the North of Argentan" be withdrawn.

Patton Is Angry

Patton protested Bradley's order to no avail. Originally, he had not been in favor of Bradley's plan to close the Falaise Gap. Patton, like Montgomery, believed that a wider encirclement to the Seine River would be more effective in cutting off the German forces west of the river. However, once committed to Bradley's plan, Patton could not understand why the gap between his forces and those of the Canadian First Army was not going to be closed. He knew the Germans would employ this opening to withdraw their forces from the area west of the Falaise Gap.

Patton asked Bradley if he could be permitted to seal off the Falaise Gap with the XV Corps, but was refused. On August 14, Bradley, without consulting Montgomery, ordered Patton's XV to send two divisions east toward the Seine River. Bradley incorrectly believed that some German units had already escaped through the Falaise Gap and wanted Patton's XV Corps to cut them off before they could cross the Seine River. Pictured is an American M-4A1 Sherman tank, armed with a 76-mm gun, crossing a burning French field.
National Archives

The Germans first began withdrawing their units eastward from the Falaise Pocket on August 16. The area in which they were trapped was close to 40 miles long and averaged between 11 and 15 miles wide. By the evening of August 18, the German forces remaining in the Falaise Pocket were confined to an area about six miles deep and seven miles wide. During the night of August 18, the Allies began an intense artillery barrage aimed at the German units still remaining in the Falaise Pocket. Pictured is an American 105-mm howitzer firing at German positions. *National Archives*

The destructive power of the aerial and artillery fire aimed at the German forces trapped in the Falaise Pocket was terrible. A First Army report described it in these terms, "The carnage wrought during the final days by the artillery of two Allied armies and the massed air forces was perhaps the greatest of the war." Pictured is an abandoned Soviet 122-mm field gun, employed by the Germans in France, where it was captured by American troops. *Patton Museum*

Beginning on the afternoon of August 16, anywhere from 20,000 to 40,000 German troops (minus most of their heavy equipment) drove through the Falaise Gap. Losses among the fleeing German troops numbered roughly 10,000 men killed with another 50,000 taken prisoner by the various Allied armies.

Bradley, in conjunction with Eisenhower, had decided for many different reasons that he did not want the XV Corps to continue its advance on to Falaise. One reason was the fear that the XV Corps would overrun the boundary lines of the Canadian First Army coming from the other direction. To the layman, the importance Bradley attached to preserving army group boundary lines seems misplaced. To the military minded, however, the establishment of boundary lines in wartime is crucial in preventing both confusion and friendly fire losses.

Another important reason Bradley and Eisenhower halted the XV Corps' advance lay in the corps' very extended position. Both long flanks of the XV Corps lay exposed to German counterattacks. Haislip had expressed his concern to Patton about this problem and received a confirmation that it would be addressed. Patton had planned to employ two newly arrived divisions of the XX Corps to provide flank protection for the advance to Argentan and Falaise. Unfortunately, for different reasons, neither of the XX Corps' divisions arrived in time.

Eisenhower and Bradley feared that once the German forces west of the Falaise Gap realized their dire predicament, they would turn eastward and overrun Patton's XV Corps in order to escape through the Falaise Gap. In his postwar memoirs, Bradley wrote that he was reluctant to send Patton's troops past Argentan because he preferred "a solid shoulder at Argen-

The three divisions of Patton's XV Corps, left behind at Argentan, finally linked up with Canadian First Army units on August 20. By the afternoon of August 21, there were no more German soldiers left to escape the Falaise Pocket, except for a few stragglers. The Falaise Gap was officially closed by the American and Canadian forces on August 22. Pictured are American soldiers riding on an M-29 cargo carrier, leading a column of German soldiers into captivity. *National Archives*

tan rather than a broken neck at Falaise." Bradley also believed that Allied artillery and tank fire, as well as air attacks, could destroy the German forces in the Falaise Pocket, while at the same time minimizing American casualties. By employing such methods, Bradley thought it would be unnecessary for the American and Canadian forces to physically meet. In hindsight, some military historians see Bradley's decision not to close the Falaise Gap as an important tactical error.

Patton's preferred means of transportation around his Third Army was an open jeep. To make sure that his men knew of his presence, the jeeps he normally traveled in were equipped with loud horns and pennants. The pennants, as seen here on one of Patton's wartime jeeps, displayed his three stars, as well as the Third Army emblem. Patton's personal driver for the entire war was Master Sergeant John L. Mims. *Patton Museum*

During his army's drive across France, Patton learned of a badly damaged B-17 bomber that had crashed in the Third Army sector. When informed the crew had survived and were at a local railroad station, Patton rushed to visit the men. On his arrival at the railroad station, Patton quickly decorated all nine men on the spot with the Bronze Star, and told them, "You've done a swell job." He also had the entire crew flown back to England in his own personal C-47 plane.
Patton Museum

Patton, seen here at center, is flanked by Eisenhower and Bradley on the right and three of his Third Army corps commanders on the left. The two-star general to the far left of the picture is Major General Manton S. Eddy, commander of Patton's XII Corps. To the right of Eddy is Major General Walton H. Walker, commander of Patton's XX Corps. Walker had a number of nicknames, including "Johnnie Walker" and "Bulldog Walker." Walker was a great admirer of his boss and imitated Patton in his style of leadership.
Patton Museum

This map shows the advance of the Allied Armies toward the Seine River and Paris in mid-August 1944. Elements of Patton's Third Army first crossed the Seine on August 19. On August 18, the citizens of Paris rose up in revolt against the occupying German forces. Paris was liberated on August 25, with the help of the 2nd Free French Armored Division as well as other Allied units. *U.S. Army map*

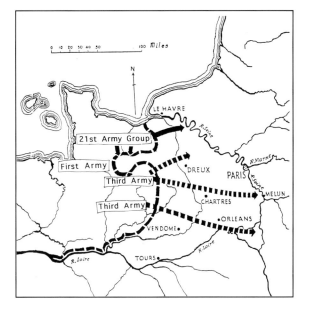

In his postwar memoirs, Bradley pointed the finger of blame at Montgomery for "his" decision not to close the Falaise Gap. Such finger pointing is very common in postwar memoirs of military leaders trying to explain wartime mistakes. Bradley wrote that he and Patton had doubted "Monty's ability to close the gap at Argentan" from the North, and they had "waited impatiently" for word from Montgomery to continue the XV Corps' advance. The unanswered question, though, is why did Bradley choose not to ask Montgomery's permission to cross his army's group boundary lines?

Patton wrote that "XV Corps could have easily entered Falaise and completely closed the gap . . . this halt was a great mistake, as I was certain that we could have entered Falaise and I

Patton's XV Corps left part of its forces at Argentan to contain the Germans in the Falaise Pocket, and started the wider envelopment to the Seine River on August 15. The other corps of Patton's Third Army (the XX and XII), located farther south, were also driving to the Seine, sweeping clear the vast area north of the Loire River. Pictured is an American M-10 tank destroyer leading a column of American infantrymen to the Seine. The soldier in the foreground has a 2.36-inch bazooka slung over his shoulder. *National Archives*

was not certain the British would." Some post-war historians and writers have professed strong doubts that Patton's XV Corps could have survived long against the experienced and battle-hardened German units trying to escape through the Falaise Gap.

On August 16, Montgomery finally phoned Bradley and suggested that Patton's XV Corps and the First Canadian Army meet, not somewhere between Argentan and Falaise, but seven miles northeast of Argentan. Since the XV Corps headquarters staff had already moved east toward the Seine River (on August 15) with the bulk of the corps, there remained nobody to direct the American part of the planned meeting. The American advance, therefore, did not begin until August 19. Patton's XV Corps finally linked up with the Canadian First Army troops on August 20, and the Gap was not officially closed until August 25.

Patton's Drive to the Seine

Although ordered by Bradley to halt on August 13, Patton continued to lobby him to keep moving. Bradley's stand-fast order made little sense to the older general. To Patton, there existed only one tactical principle, "To use the means at hand to inflict the maximum amount of wounds, death, and destruction on the enemy in the minimum amount of time."

With Patton's prompting, Bradley issued new orders to the XV Corps on August 14, to send the 5th Armored Division and the 79th Infantry Division eastward in the direction of an area north of Paris along the Seine River. The Free French 2nd Armored Division and 90th Infantry Division remained behind in the Argentan area.

By sending the XV Corps north of Paris to the Seine, Patton's Third Army would, in effect, be extending another trap around any German troops that managed to escape eastward out of the Falaise Pocket. In addition, the Third Army could cut off any remaining German forces west of the Seine that were not trapped in the Falaise Pocket. The Allies estimated, on August 19, that

American troops of the 28th Infantry Division march down the Champs Elysee during a victory parade in Paris on August 29. On August 27, Eisenhower ordered food, fuel, and medical supplies delivered to Paris. These supplies were the only source of subsistence for the city for the six weeks after its liberation. The Free French 2nd Armored Division rejoined Patton's Third Army on September 8. *National Archives*

75,000 German troops and 250 tanks could still be encircled west of the Seine River.

As Patton's various corps headed toward the Seine, the citizens of Paris rose up against their German oppressors. Knowing the Allied armies would head in the general direction of the city, French Resistance leaders inside Paris radioed for help before the Germans could destroy the city. Roughly 20,000 German soldiers guarded Paris, most of whom were positioned on the western outskirts of the city with 20 batteries of 88-mm antiaircraft guns. Within the actual city, General Dietrich von Choltitz, the German commander, had about 5,000 men and a small assortment of tanks, armored cars, and artillery pieces. Facing incredible political pressure to liberate Paris, Eisenhower gave permission for the Free French 2nd Armored Division to capture the city. In its advance the French armored division had support from various First Army units as well as a contingent of British troops. The German commander of Paris surrendered the city on August 25.

On its advance to the Seine, the XV Corps

Opposite: As the Allied Armies approached the Seine River the citizens of Paris attempted an armed revolt against the German forces occupying their city. The revolt was not encouraged by the Allies, who were in no hurry to liberate the city. If they liberated the city they would have to provide its inhabitants with food, coal, gas, and electricity. Allied military supply lines were already badly strained at the time. Eisenhower could not ignore the French uprising in Paris. After much deliberation, and political pressure from the French, Eisenhower decided to send the Free French 2nd Armored Division of Patton's Third Army, and the American 4th Infantry Division to help liberate the city from the Germans on August 23. Two days later the German commander of Paris surrendered the city. Pictured is an American M-8 armored car passing the Arc de Triumph after the liberation of the city. *National Archives*

Two American soldiers display the original 2.36-inch model bazooka M-1 (on the left) and the later, improved version designated the M-9 (on the right). The M-9 version of the bazooka was constructed out of aluminum, thereby weighing five pounds less than the original steel version. Both versions of the bazooka proved useful not only against armored vehicles, but also against enemy troops inside buildings or pillboxes. *National Archives*

The first hint of a looming logistical crisis for Patton's Third Army appeared in early August. The main problem was the supply services not having enough trucks to keep up with Patton's fast-moving divisions. The most numerous truck in the U.S. Army's inventory during the war was the 2 1/2-ton truck 6x6, of which American factories built over 800,000 by 1945. The vehicle pictured is a GMC-built version belonging to a private collector. *Author photo*

met only minor German resistance, which so encouraged Bradley that he gave permission for the 79th Infantry Division to cross the Seine on August 19. The division built a temporary Bailey bridge across the river that opened to traffic on August 23. At the same time, the 5th Armored Division drove up the western bank of the Seine, cutting German escape routes.

Despite the best American efforts, the Germans managed to move 20,000 men and some wheeled vehicles across the Seine to its eastern bank between August 20 and 24, using ferries and boats. What the Germans could not save were their tanks. Of the roughly 2,300 tanks committed to battle west of the Seine since the beginning of the Allied invasion in June, fewer than 120 managed to make it back to the east bank of the Seine in late August.

In the original Overlord plans, the Allied armies planned to stop at the Seine so they

Due to logistical problems that prevented the Third Army from receiving all its needed supplies, Bradley wanted to stop Patton's forces short of the Seine River. Weak German opposition in front of the Third Army, however, proved too much of a temptation for Bradley. On August 17, he gave Patton permission to drive on to the Seine. To conserve gasoline and other supplies, Patton left the XII Corps behind to catch up later. Pictured are American soldiers filling up thousands of five-gallon "jerry cans" with gasoline from a line of fuel tankers. *National Archives*

On August 19, Patton ordered the 5th Armored Division of his XV Corps to clear the west bank of the Seine River in its sector. Patton's intention was to deny the German forces still west of the Seine suitable crossing points across the river. Almost immediately the 5th Armored Division ran into stiff German opposition. Fog and rain that continued for several days protected the German units from Allied fighter bombers. Pictured is a burning M-4 Sherman tank caught in a German ambush. *National Archives*

It would take the 5th Armored Division five days of hard fighting to advance about 20 miles and accomplish its mission. Pictured is a knocked-out American M-4 Sherman tank that took a German high-velocity round right through the gun mantle. The Sherman, with only three inches of armor on its front and two inches on its sides, proved extremely vulnerable to the entire range of German late war antitank weapons. *National Archives*

could reorganize and build up a supply base. Once this job was finished, they would then continue their advance across France to the German border. This plan would be forgotten as an incredible spirit of optimism began to sweep through the higher ranks of the Allied Armies. On August 26, Eisenhower's headquarters issued a summary that stated, "Two and a half months of bitter fighting . . . have brought the end of the war in Europe within sight, almost within reach. The strength of the German Armies in the West has been shattered. Paris belongs to France again, and the Allied armies are streaming toward the frontiers of the Reich."

With the 5th Armored Division pushing up the western bank of the Seine, Bradley faced the problem once again of having to cross Montgomery's 21st Army Group boundary lines. Having learned a painful lesson from what had happened at the Falaise Gap, Bradley quickly asked and received Montgomery's permission to continue the 5th Armored Division's advance. On August 20, Montgomery reaffirmed his desire to push the Allied armies forward by issuing an order that cautioned: "This is no time to relax, or to sit back and congratulate ourselves. . . . Let us finish off the business in record time." On August 24, Bradley ordered the XV Corps transferred from the Third Army to the First Army command.

Before Bradley ordered part of the XV Corps eastward toward the Seine on August 14, Patton had already ordered his other corps, the XII and XX, in the same general direction as the XV Corps, with the Seine as their ultimate objective. The XII Corps consisted of the 4th Armored Division and the 35th Infantry Division. The XX Corps consisted of the 7th Armored Division commanded by Major General Lindsay M. Sylvester and the 5th Infantry Division. Before reaching the Seine, both corps had to secure an intermediate objective known as the Paris-Orleans Gap.

The Paris-Orleans Gap lay between the city of Paris on the Seine River and the city of Orleans on the Loire River. It was the only land route available to the Germans that did not require the crossing of any major rivers or bridges. Allied air power had destroyed almost all the bridges across the Seine and Loire Rivers. By securing the Paris-Orleans Gap, the Third Army could deny the German Seventh and Fifth Panzer Armies a possible escape route to southern France.

Not wasting time, Patton's VII Corps captured Orleans, the southern anchor of the Paris-Orleans Gap, on the night of August 16. Due to supply problems Patton held the XII Corps at Orleans until August 21. The speed of the XII Corps advance prevented any German hopes of organizing a defense of the Paris-Orleans Gap.

On the night of August 19, a battalion of infantry-men from the Third Army's XV Corps first crossed the Seine River over a small and narrow dam. By the next morning, additional infantrymen began cross-ing the Seine in small wooden M-2 assault boats, as pictured. Army engineers soon set about building a large pontoon bridge to allow wheeled and tracked vehicles to cross the river. *National Archives*

To protect the southern flank that rested on the Loire River, Patton again employed planes of the XIX TAC to patrol on the southern side of the Loire River and watch for any signs of Ger-man counterattacks. As an added measure of security, Patton ordered the XII Corps to clear the northern bank of the Loire River and destroy any remaining bridges. On the evening of August 25, elements of the XII Corps crossed the Seine River near the city of Troyes.

The XX Corps, located north of the XII Corps and south of the XV Corps, received orders from Patton on August 14 to capture Chartres. The city of Chartres lay directly in the center of the Paris-Orleans Gap. It had a popu-lation of 40,000 people and the nickname "The Gateway to Paris." The 7th Armored Division reached the outskirts of the city on August 15. Early the next morning the division raced into the heart of the city. Heavy fighting developed, with American armored infantrymen slugging it out with the tenacious students of a Luft-waffe antiaircraft training school. The corps' mechanized cavalry group swung around the town in an arc and prevented the escape of the German garrison.

Savage counterattacks drove the tankers and armored infantrymen of the 7th Armored Division back. Facing the loss of the newly liberated city, Walker quickly rushed ele-ments of the 5th Infantry Division into Chartres. Large and still-organized German troops fought from the woods south of Chartres and in the city itself. Despite their best efforts, the German garrison surrendered on August 19. Two days later in a steady rain, the XX Corps set out for the 60-mile drive to the Seine.

On reaching the Seine the next day the XX Corps found the east bank of the river heavily

In a desperate search for extra protection, American tank crews began adding a variety of materials to the outsides of their tanks, such as sandbags, logs, wood, rocks, and even cement. The purpose of these materials was to hopefully explode or deflect the shaped charge warheads of German antitank weapons like the Panzerfaust. Pictured is an Ameri-can M-5A1 light tank whose crew has welded spare track links to the front hull of their vehicle. This vehicle also mounts a Culin hedgerow-cutting device on the lower front hull. *National Archives*

defended by over 18,000 German soldiers with a large number of artillery units. Documents taken from dead or captured enemy soldiers showed the Germans had hopes of delaying or possibly holding the hard-charging XX Corps

From August 20 till August 25, Patton's XII and XX Corps managed to establish four bridgeheads across the Seine River. Pictured is a 57-mm antitank gun M-1 being ferried across the Seine River. By September 1, both the XII and the XX Corps got across the Meuse River. Unfortunately, Army planners had never anticipated the speed of Patton's advance across France, and were not prepared to support it with all the supplies it needed. *National Archives*

along the river. There was no other American bridgehead across the Seine south of Paris. Despite repeated attempts, the 7th Armored Division could not push through the constant German artillery barrages. During the evening of the 22nd, air support bombed the German defensive positions.

Early next morning, Walker began a multi-prong attack along the Seine. In one area, American infantrymen crossed by either swimming or rowing abandoned boats across the river. The Germans quickly counterattacked the soldiers who made it to the shore. With the full support of corps artillery units, the American units managed to cling to their small bridgehead. In another area, two battalions of XX Corps swam and waded across a ford to rout the surprised German defenders on the east side of the river.

Army engineers quickly built temporary bridges or employed small ferries to bring additional troops and equipment across.

On August 26, elements of the 5th Infantry Division swept along the west bank of the Seine to capture the town of Nogent-sur-Seine from a German panzer grenadier division. Sadly, the bridge across the Seine they sought was destroyed by the Germans prior to their arrival. In an all-night operation, the corps engineers erected a new bridge across the Seine.

The German ground forces had lost over 400,000 killed, wounded, or captured fighting in the west. In addition, 200,000 other German troops became prisoners of war. More than 1,300 tanks, 20,000 other vehicles, 500 assault guns, and 1,500 field guns and heavier artillery pieces were captured or destroyed. The German

The first pontoon bridge across the Seine was completed by Army engineers on the afternoon of August 20. The bulk of the 79th Infantry Division, including tanks, artillery, and tank destroyers, was on the eastern bank of the Seine by that evening. Pictured is an American M-10 tank destroyer, crossing the Seine on a pontoon bridge. In 1939, there were only 6,576 engineers in the entire regular Army. By May 1945, the Army Engineers had reached a strength of 688,182 men. *National Archives*

Third Army antiaircraft units were hurriedly emplaced around the first bridge across the Seine River to protect it from aerial attack. The American antiaircraft gunners shot down a dozen German planes on their first day. After four days of guarding the bridge, they accounted for a total of 50 German aircraft. Pictured is an American Army 40-mmM-1 antiaircraft gun. The 40-mmM-1 fired a two-pound shell up to 11,000 feet. A well-trained gun crew could fire up to 120 rounds per minute. *National Archives*

Hitler was furious when he found out that Patton's Third Army had managed to cross the Seine River. He ordered that every effort be made to stop the Americans as quickly as possible. Unfortunately for Hitler, what remained of the German ground forces that escaped from the Falaise Pocket were in no shape to mount an effective defensive operation. Pictured is an American soldier posing next to a destroyed German Mark IV medium tank fitted with a wire-mesh antitank bazooka screen along its hull. *National Archives*

In the initial plans for the invasion of France and the drive toward Germany, the Allied planners had counted on using the French railroad system to bring supplies forward. The widespread destruction inflicted on the French railroads by Allied planes and the French Resistance made this very difficult. The Army Corps of Engineers and the Transportation Corps were assigned the mission of restoring the French rail system. Pictured are French railroad officials looking at a marshaling yard wrecked by Allied bombs. *National Archives*

Through hard work, the Americans managed to restore two main railroad lines from the Normandy area to the outskirts of Paris by August 30. The damage to the rail yards around Paris and the destroyed Seine River bridges made further progress much harder to continue. Another problem that prevented the effective use of the French railroad system was the widespread destruction of French locomotives and rolling stock. Pictured are two French railroad workers examining a locomotive that had fallen into a large bomb crater. *National Archives*

Air Force took a fearful beating. At least 2,370 planes were destroyed in the air and 1,167 on the ground.

Supplying the Third Army

The Third Army's problems with logistical support began with the turn eastward toward the Seine on August 3. In chasing the fleeing German military forces across France, logistical considerations became subordinated to prospects of a quick victory. As a result, by the end of August, almost 90 percent of all the American supplies remained near the invasion beaches. Between these beachhead supply dumps and forward army depots (often a distance of 300 miles), there were few stockpiles

capable of supporting large units conducting sustained operations.

In their initial post-invasion plans, American commanders had hoped to use the French railroad system to move supplies forward to their advancing armies. Unfortunately, the combination of air attacks and sabotage by the French Resistance rendered the railroad system almost completely useless, forcing logistical commanders to depend on trucks to supply the forward elements of the fast-moving Third Army. They soon established a temporary long-distance highway system that came to be immortalized as "The Red Ball Express."

The Red Ball Express officially began on August 25, and lasted until November 15.

To overcome the supply problems that were hampering the Third Army, a temporary system known as the Red Ball Express was instituted. The Army's supply service devised a circular one-way truck route across France. it operated from the original invasion beaches to the fighting zone and back again. Between August 25 and September 5, the Red Ball Express brought 89,000 tons of supplies up to the Third Army. *National Archives*

Within five days of its inception, the Express reached its peak operational level, with 6,000 trucks delivering 12,342 tons of supplies to the Third Army. Operating 24 hours a day, the truckers drove on special one-way roads that remained off-limits to all other military traffic. The roads themselves were marked with large red balls to guide the truck convoys to their drop-off points so the truckers would not need to stop and check maps.

The most important item delivered in the early stages was gasoline. To supply enough trucks to keep the Red Ball Express rolling,

many newly arrived combat troops as well as units classified as nonessential (such as antiaircraft and heavy artillery) were stripped of their wheeled transports. In addition to the truck convoys, the Allies also employed transport planes and converted bombers to move supplies forward to their various armies. Due to low tonnage capacity, support handling, and weather, airlifted supplies remained fairly low.

The Drive beyond the Seine

As Patton crossed the Seine River, Eisenhower began thinking about the future direc-

Above: Among the most crucial supplies needed by the American armies in their fast-moving advance across France was gasoline. During the week of August 20, the First and Third Armies consumed 800,000 gallons of gasoline. The overloaded trucks of the Red Ball Express alone consumed more than 300,000 gallons per day, and wore out tires at an incredible rate. Pictured is a tire storage site in France in late 1944. *National Archives*

tion of the war. The Ruhr, the heart of Germany's industrial might, lay within striking distance of France and remained the Allies' primary objective. Berlin, the capital of Germany and an important political objective, lay too far east.

Once Eisenhower decided that the Ruhr was his main target, he figured out which of four routes from northern France was the most suitable for his forces. Ruling out both the easily flooded flatlands of Flanders and the hilly woodlands of the Ardennes, Eisenhower chose to divide his forces into two mutually supporting groups for the advance on Germany's Ruhr. Due to fuel shortfalls, he also had to face the fact that the Allied logistical system could not fully support the advance of both Mont-

By the end of August, Patton's Third Army had captured the city of Verdun and was across the Meuse River. From the east side of the Meuse, Patton could drive on to the Moselle River, and possibly capture the French cities of Metz and Nancy. From this area, Patton would be within striking distance of the Rhine River in Germany. All Patton needed was enough fuel to keep his tanks moving. Pictured is a squad of American infantrymen being briefed on their next mission. Behind the soldiers is a heavily sandbagged M-5A1 light tank. *National Archives*

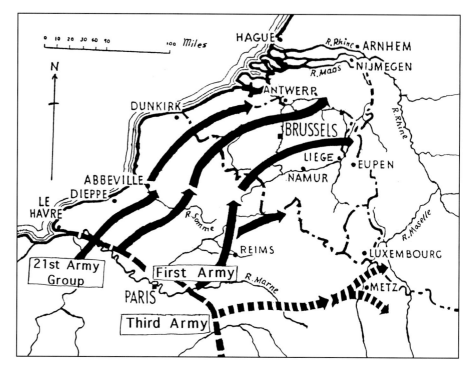

This map shows the advance of the Allied Armies beyond the Seine River in August and September 1944. The advance of Montgomery's 21st Army Group received priority over the advance of Bradley's 12th Army Group for many different reasons. They included the chance of capturing the large, and badly needed, ports of Antwerp and Rotterdam. Other reasons included the overrunning of German V-1 and V-2 rocket sites and a more favorable route to Germany and its industrial heart, the Ruhr. *U.S. Army map*

The British forces under Montgomery's 21st Army Group captured the large and badly needed inland port city of Antwerp on September 4. Unfortunately, Montgomery's troops failed to secure the 65-mile water route to the city until early November 1944. The Germans took advantage of this major tactical error, and ferried over 100,000 men of their Fifteenth Army to safety. Pictured is the proud crew of a British M-4A4 Sherman tank showing off a captured German flag. *British Army Tank Museum*

gomery's 21st Army Group and Bradley's 12th Army Group. Eisenhower decided after much deliberation that the main Allied effort would be with Montgomery's 21st Army Group. Montgomery's forces would advance in a northeasterly direction through the cities of Amiens, Manbeuge, and Liege along the northern edge of the Ardennes in Belgium. This route was both favorable to the advance of large military forces as well as being the most direct route to the Ruhr. In such an advance, Montgomery's army group would liberate both Belgium and parts of the Netherlands. The large and badly needed ports of Antwerp and Rotterdam would also fall into Allied hands. Most important, Montgomery's forces would overrun the German "V" rocket sites. From these launching sites, Germany had unleashed its rocket weapons at England in large numbers, taking a heavy toll on British lives and morale.

The secondary Allied effort would consist of Bradley's 12th Army Group. The Ninth Army took on the job of capturing Brest and other French ports. The advance of the First and Third Armies also lay in a northeasterly direction, but to the south of the Ardennes in Belgium. The Third Army advance called for the capture of the cities of Metz and Nancy before moving on to the Rhine River. The path to these cities was less favorable for an advance of a large military force than that north of the Ardennes.

The great advance across France by the Allied Armies began to lose its momentum in the first week of September, as their supply lines became intolerably stretched. Eisenhower was forced to put a brake on the southern advance of the American Armies in order to devote all the Allied logistical support system to the northern advance of Montgomery's 21st Army Group. Pictured is a British soldier, armed with the well-known No. 4 Mark I Lee-Enfield rifle, peering out at his surroundings from a ruined building. *Patton Museum*

It was also a far less direct route, since it did not lead directly to the Ruhr but instead to the Saar Basin, which had a much smaller industrial capacity than the Ruhr.

The very difficult decisions made by Eisenhower on the future direction of the war managed to upset almost everyone. Montgomery felt that all the Allied forces should come under his command for one massive thrust into Germany. Eisenhower could not agree since American public opinion would no longer allow the growing number of American armies to remain under British command. Eisenhower took over the job as commander of all Allied ground forces in western Europe from Montgomery on September 1.

Both Bradley and Patton were livid over what they perceived as Eisenhower's decision to favor the British effort under Montgomery rather than the planned advance of Bradley's 12th Army Group. Patton was so upset that he tried to persuade Bradley to quit in protest of Eisenhower's decision. Bradley declined Patton's suggestion. Patton remained convinced that such a threat would force Eisenhower to change his mind. Since the invasion of North Africa in November 1942, Patton often voiced the opinion that Eisenhower favored the British more than his own people. At one point, Patton wrote, "Monty does what he pleases, and Ike says, 'Yes, Sir!'"

At the same time Patton cursed Eisenhower's decision, his Third Army's XII and XX Corps continued to enlarge their bridgeheads across the Seine River to favor Montgomery's advance. To flesh out his corps he added an infantry division to each, the 80th going to the XII Corps and the 90th going to the XX Corps.

On August 31, the gas tanks of Patton's Third Army began running dry. The Germans used this respite to build up their defensive positions. Beginning on September 4, gas once more began flowing into the Third Army's vehicles. Elements of Patton's Third Army quickly crossed the Moselle River, north of the French city of Nancy, on September 5. Other elements of the Third Army crossed the Moselle south of the French city of Metz on September 8. Pictured is an American-built M-3A3 light tank, employed by the Free French 2nd Armored Division, as part of Patton's Third Army. *National Archives*

Patton's VIII Corps, still fighting in Brittany, was not available for the eastward drive.

On September 5 the VIII Corps became part of the Ninth Army, but the 83rd Infantry Division and 6th Armored Division remained with Patton. To make up for the loss of the VIII Corps, Bradley transferred the XV Corps headquarters from First Army back to Third Army control, but without any attached divisions. Bradley later sent the 79th and 90th Infantry Divisions, and the Free French 2nd Armored Division to fill out the XV Corps. Due to the delay in receiving the divisions, the XV Corps did not become available for Patton's initial eastward advance. It did see action on the southern flank of the Third Army between September 11 through September 20.

To reach Metz and Nancy, the Third Army would have to first cross the Marne and Meuse Rivers. Units of both the XII and XX Corps crossed on August 28, in the face of weak German resistance. The XII Corps breached the Meuse River three days later. Patton was now in position to attack toward the Moselle River and the French cities of Metz and Nancy. If these cities fell, the Third Army would be barely 100 miles away from the Rhine. But, to the chagrin of the bold commander, his tanks had no more fuel to continue the advance.

Left: Pictured together in Europe are Eisenhower and Montgomery. During early September 1944, they began a long series of debates (sometimes heated) about the future strategy of the war. Beside talking about strategy, both leaders had to address the national interests of each of their respective countries. These national interests did not always coincide, which led to a certain level of conflict between the various Allied political and military leaders in 1944 and 1945. *National Archives*

Once across the Moselle River, Patton firmly believed that his divisions would quickly roll up the German defensive positions and thrust forward to the Rhine River. The only barrier Patton foresaw on the way to the Rhine was the German defensive fortifications known as the West Wall or "Siegfried Line." The West Wall consisted of a long belt (of varying depth) of pillboxes, minefields, and concrete tank traps (nicknamed "Dragon's teeth" by the Germans). *National Archives*

Bradley's 12th Army Group informed the 3rd Army on August 30 that gasoline stocks were running low and that no additional fuel would be forthcoming until September 3. The lack of a strong logistical support system was finally catching up with Patton. To make matters worse, Eisenhower explained that all available fuel supplies would go to Montgomery's 21st Army Group until further notice. Eisenhower also informed Patton that he could not continue his advance until sufficient stocks of gasoline arrived.

The Germans saw this pause in the Third Army's lightning advance across France as a gift and quickly rushed in reinforcements to oppose any future Third Army attack. A very angry Patton wrote, "Eisenhower kept talking of the future Great Battle of Germany while we

assured him that the Germans have nothing left to fight with and if we push on now, there will be a Great Battle of Germany. . . . God deliver us from our friends. We can handle the enemy."

No one knew it yet, but the grand advance of the Third Army across France that began with Operation Cobra in late July was at its end. Patton and the Third Army would now face 16 weeks of slow and bloody fighting in what military historians would refer to (unofficially) as "The Lorraine Campaign."

At the end of the war, Patton summarized his feeling about the Third Army advance being halted by Eisenhower: "(I) feel that had I been permitted to go all out, the war would have ended sooner and more lives would have been saved. Particularly I think this statement applies to the time when, early in September, we

Patton's hope of seeing his Third Army make a quick thrust to the Rhine River was quickly dashed. A number of factors led to this lack of success, including more fuel shortages, difficult terrain, bad weather, and stiff German resistance. Hitler had ordered that the area in front of the West Wall be held at all costs. Pictured are American soldiers, escorting a group of German prisoners, passing a destroyed (and burned out) M-4A3 Sherman tank that took a nasty hit in its turret. *National Archives*

were halted, owning to the desire, or the necessity, on the part of General Eisenhower in backing Montgomery's move to the North. At the time there was no question of doubt that we could have gone through and across the Rhine within ten days."

Patton, always optimistic, had overlooked the geography of the Lorraine area. Unlike the flat plains of northern France, which contained an extensive road network ideal for armored operation, the military topography of the Lorraine area was both hilly and contained few roads that led to the Saar Basin and the Rhine River, making it less than ideal for large-scale armored operations. Another factor ignored by Patton was the impact that the weather would have on his plans.

In postwar testimony, the Chief of Staff of the IX Engineer Command responsible for building and maintaining airfields in Europe during World War II answered Patton's claim of being able to reach Germany in ten days by declaring, "Had Patton continued through the Saar Valley and the Vosges it would have been without close air support and with a very small contribution in the way of air supply beyond the Reims-Epernay line. . . . I don't doubt that we could have carried about two armored and one motorized division up to Köln [the German city of Cologne], but then where? Certainly not across the Rhine. A good task force of Panzerfaust, manned by Hitler Youth, could have finished them off before they reached Kassel."

The biggest thorn in Patton's side during the Lorraine Campaign was the capture of the old French fortress city of Metz. Pictured are American soldiers using a captured German 88-mm Pak.43 gun (on a cruciform antitank mount) to fire at Metz. The city of Metz was defended by more than 30 large concrete and steel forts. Despite the age of the forts, most of which dated from World War I, they were proof against most Allied weapons. *National Archives*

Patton Plans a New Offensive

On September 5, with gasoline once more flowing into the Third Army's fuel tanks, Patton ordered the XII and XX Corps into action. The XII Corps received the job of seizing the city of Nancy in preparation for an advance to the Rhine River. Nancy lay 35 miles south of Metz and was historically the ruling city of Lorraine. It was also an important transportation center for both road and rail. The 35th Infantry Division, XII Corps, got the job of guarding the southern flank of the Third Army's advance until the XV Corps could arrive.

At this point, the XX Corps consisted of the 7th Armored Division and two infantry divisions, the 5th and 90th. Their main job involved crossing the Moselle River, and from there, the

Saar River some 30 miles east of the Moselle. The two old fortified cities that formed the anchor position for the main German defensive line, Metz and Thionville, were to be intermediate objectives. The ultimate objective of the XX Corps, like the XII Corps, remained the Rhine River.

On the eve of the attack, Patton (like his superiors) did not foresee any major German resistance. Patton himself had expressed the opinion that the German forces in front of the Third Army might make a stand at or in front of the West Wall, but he was confident that it could be breached by armor. Among the senior Allied military staff, many believed Patton would reach the Rhine by the middle of December. On September 7, Patton told a group of

An unwelcome sight for any American tanker in Europe during the last two years of the war was this view of a German Jagdpanther. The Jagdpanther was armed with a high-velocity 88-mm gun (Pak.43), mounted on the heavily modified, turretless chassis of a Panther medium tank. Production of the Jagdpanther began in January 1944, with only 392 built before the end of the war. They were deployed with Army antitank units. *Frank Schulz collection*

Third Army correspondents in reference to his new offensive, "I hope to go through the Siegfried Line [West Wall] like shit through a goose."

The West Wall was basically a series of pill-boxes, minefields, and tank traps, varying in depth, and it extended from the southeastern corner of the Netherlands all the way down to the Swiss frontier. Built before the German conquest of France, the West Wall had fallen into disrepair and was somewhat outdated. In a belated attempt to upgrade and rearm the Wall, Hitler ordered 200,000 German civilians to assist in repairing it in August. By December, the Germans did succeed in somewhat

strengthening the West Wall. One of the best-defended areas existed directly in front of the planned Third Army advance.

The lightning advance across France in August, and the spectacle of a fleeing German military had lulled the American Army leaders into a false sense of superiority. The Germans still had a lot of fight left. Hitler began planning for a large-scale counterattack against Patton's Third Army as early as August 28.

Directly facing Patton's Third Army in early September were seven understrength infantry divisions and a panzer brigade of the German First Army. The advance of the Third Army toward the Moselle would also brush against

The M-3 was commonly referred to by most soldiers by its popular nickname, the "grease gun." The weapon weighed a little over eight pounds and fired a .45-caliber slug from a 30-round detachable box magazine. It was designed as a cheap-to-build replacement for the complex and costly M-1 Thompson sub-machine gun. American factories built more than 600,000 grease guns during the war. *National Archives*

the northern flank of the German 19th Army, consisting of seven understrength divisions.

In a series of meetings Hitler instructed Generalfeldmarschall Walter Model, the German commander of the Western Front, that he wanted a large counterattack launched at the southern flank of Patton's Third Army as soon as possible. Hitler also instructed his commanders that he wanted the German armies to stand and hold in front of the West Wall at all costs.

Due to the static nature of the fighting on the Western front, in September 1944 the German Army began using land lines for the majority of its communication needs instead of radios. This change in German communication habits effectively robbed the Allies of Ultra's valuable insights on many German plans. As a result, Allied ground operations made much less progress between September and December 1944 compared to the period between July and August 1944.

Chapter Five

THE LORRAINE CAMPAIGN

Patton was unaware of the German buildup or plans to delay the Third Army in the Lorraine sector. Major General Manton S. Eddy, the XII Corps commander, ordered a surprise crossing of the Moselle River north of Nancy by the 80th Infantry Division on the morning of September 5. According to information provided by the local French resistance and cavalry patrols, the German defenders were unable to put up much of a fight. In actuality, the Germans were well aware of the XII Corps plans and had two strong panzer grenadier divisions deployed in the area. The Germans cut the 80th Infantry Division to pieces. By the next day, any American soldiers on the east bank of the Moselle River not killed or taken prisoner were withdrawn and the attack canceled.

With his attack north of the city being repelled, Eddy decided to make the area south of Nancy the corps' main effort. He ordered the 35th Infantry Division and 4th Armored Division to advance on Nancy from the south. Due to the influence of Wood, the 4th Armored Division commander, Eddy, modified his plans at the last minute. The 35th Infantry Division and the bulk of the 4th Armored Division would still make the main effort south of Nancy, but the 80th Infantry Division would also attempt another crossing north of the city. Elements of the 4th Armored Division would stand by in reserve, ready to exploit an opportunity in either direction. If the northern crossing succeeded, Nancy would fall in a pincer movement.

On September 10, Bradley and Patton, working together, decided to undermine Eisenhower's decision to favor Montgomery's northern advance. Their plan called for Patton to become so involved in operations across the

During the October lull in the Third Armys' operations, painful lessons learned from trying to capture Fort Driant were incorporated into new training exercises. These lessons would later be successfully applied by the Third Army in its early November offensive that finally saw the reduction of the Metz fort system. Patton is pictured in his personal M-20 armored utility car, escorting Averell Harriman, the American ambassador to the Soviet Union, on a tour of the Third Army. *Patton Museum*

Moselle River that Eisenhower would be unable to reduce their allotment of supplies for fear of an American military defeat.

On September 11, Bradley visited Eisenhower to inform him that Patton had just started to advance toward the Moselle. Bradley also told Eisenhower that if Patton's forces had not successfully crossed the Moselle by September 14, the advance would end. The next day Bradley wrote a message to Eisenhower in which he pleaded with him not to make any additional cuts in Patton's supply allotment. Eisenhower quickly convinced Bradley that sup-

Pictured is an American officer taking cover with a member of the French Resistance. The resistance was also referred to as the French Forces of the Interior (FFI). During the Third Army's advance across France, the FFI provided valuable assistance to Patton's forces. On reaching the Lorraine area of France, the FFI proved far less effective to Patton, due to the pro-German feelings of many of the area's inhabitants. *National Archives*

porting Montgomery's northern advance was the logical decision. Patton was not swayed by Bradley's change of heart and asked him not to contact him until after dark on the 19th so he could continue pushing his forces forward.

On September 11, the 35th Infantry Division managed to cross the Moselle River against stiff opposition and establish an infantry bridgehead south of Nancy. The lead elements of the 4th Armored Division's main effort chose not to wait for construction of heavy pontoon bridges. Instead, the lead tanks improvised a crossing of the drained canal flanking the Moselle, forded the river, and established con-

Patton entered the Lorraine area of France with a strong belief that the German defenses would crumble in front of his Third Army. Colonel Oscar W. Koch, Patton's G-2 (intelligence), tried to warn his boss at the end of August that the German military was still not decisively beaten. Patton dismissed Koch's warning and continued with his grand plans for a drive to the Rhine River. Pictured is a squad of German infantry on the move. *Patton Museum*

tact with the 35th Infantry Division while engineers constructed bridges behind them. Poor roads, rather than German resistance, proved to be the main impediment to the 4th's drive toward the rear of Nancy.

North of Nancy, the 80th Infantry Division mounted a successful crossing on September 12. The Germans reacted quickly with strong counterattacks, but to no avail. Despite the heavy German resistance, elements of the 4th

Hitler was very aware of the danger that an American breakthrough in the Lorraine sector would pose to Germany. By the first week of September, the reinforced First Army, facing Patton's Third Army, was the strongest German Army in the West. The German command headquarters in the West (OB West) estimated it had a combat strength equal to three panzer grenadier divisions, four and a half infantry divisions, and a single panzer brigade of roughly 60 tanks. Pictured is a German panzer grenadier checking the road ahead of his armored half-track.
Frank Schulz collection

Hitler, like Patton, had made grand plans for the opening stages of the Lorraine Campaign. As early as September 3, Hitler began planning for a large-scale counterattack directed against the exposed southern flank of Patton's forces. This decision was partly dictated by the strategic necessity for the Germans to prevent a juncture of the American Third Army with the Seventh Army coming up from southern France. Pictured are two small German reconnaissance SdKfz 250 half-tracks taking a break in a French town.
Frank Schulz collection

Armored Division rushed through the 80th Infantry Division bridgehead. The objective of the American tanks was to execute a deep attack, with the objective for the day being the capture of the important road center at Chateau-Salins, some 20 miles distant. They met little opposition until reaching Chateau-Salins the next day. The northern elements of Eddy's division therefore drove southward to the vicinity of Arracourt, cutting the German lines of communication to Nancy in the process. From the area around Arracourt, the northern elements were to continue southward until they could link up with the elements of the division advancing from the south.

On September 15, the northern elements of the 4th Armored Division began a four-day campaign of destruction behind German lines before linking up with the southern elements of the division. The raid forced the German division defending Nancy to withdraw, allowing the 35th Infantry Division to occupy the city against little opposition.

To the officers of the 4th Armored Division, there was no question as to the reunited division's next move. The obvious path of action was to exploit the advantage immediately and keep the enemy on the run. The road to Germany was open. Eddy rejected the division's request to continue its advance, because there were no provisions to support a continued armored advance. Instead, Eddy directed the armored division to turn around in order to assist the 35th and 80th Infantry Divisions in mopping-up operations.

Eddy informed the 4th Armored Division that it would be able to resume its general offensive on September 18. The attack plan

The units assigned to the planned German counterattack, aimed at Patton's Third Army, were personally selected by Hitler. They included three panzer grenadier divisions and a number of newly formed panzer brigades. Hitler also hoped to add three panzer divisions to his counterattack. Pictured is a German SdKfz 234/2 eight-wheel armored car (nicknamed the Puma) armed with a turret-mounted 50-mm gun. This particular vehicle has lost a wheel to a mine. *Frank Schulz collection*

would consist of the armored division and the 35th Infantry Division attacking in column. Bad weather forced a postponement until September 19, five days after elements of the 4th Armored Division had reached Arracourt. As a result, the attack was never launched because the Arracourt location had become endangered. The XII Corps had lost the initiative. Eddy's decision to consolidate his positions proved to be a priceless gift of time to the Germans, during which the German First Army concentrated reserves around Chateau-Salins, thus blocking one of the principal Third Army avenues to the Rhine River.

In an even more serious development, the Fifth Panzer Army began assembling forces for a major counteroffensive against the XII Corps' right flank. The German commander of the Fifth Panzer Army had orders to roll up the Third Army's right flank with a massive counterattack, but the 4th Armored Division's sudden thrust to Arracourt surprised the

The initial date set by Hitler for his counterattack against Patton's Third Army was September 12. Due to Allied pressure all along the Western Front, the Germans could not disengage the units earmarked for the counterattack, and had to postpone the operation. On September 13, one of Hitler's newly formed panzer brigades ran into the Free French 2nd Armored Division and lost 60 tanks. Here, French soldiers look over a destroyed German Panther tank (model G) that bogged down in soft soil. *National Archives*

Hitler's long-delayed counterattack against Patton's Third Army began on the morning of September 18, when advance elements of the German attack struck part of the American Fourth Armored Division. The American armored division was under the command of Major General John Shirley Wood. At first, Wood believed the German attack was only a minor nuisance attack. By the next day, Wood knew he faced a major German counterattack, and began reinforcing his units engaged with the German forces. Pictured are curious American soldiers looking over a destroyed Panther tank (model G) and a Mark IV (model J) in the background. National Archives

panzer army and threw off the effort. It also forced the Germans into a series of premature, piecemeal attacks strung out over 12 days. The first of these fell on elements of the 4th Armored Division at Lunéville on September 18. Reinforcements from the 4th and 6th Armored Divisions drove off the Germans. Both Eddy and his divisional commanders, believing the Lunéville engagement to be only a local counterattack, proceeded with plans for another corps offensive to begin the next day. Reports of increased German activity throughout the night of September 18, however, forced Eddy and his commanders to delay their attack. What had happened was the Fifth Panzer Army had simply bypassed Lunéville and was moving

north to strike at the exposed position of the 4th Armored Division around Arracourt. The resulting operation was one of the largest armored engagements ever fought on the Western Front.

Under the cover of the early morning fog on September 19, the Germans launched their first large tank attack against elements of the 4th Armored Division in the Arracourt area. In a series of sharp and violent engagements, the American tankers outmaneuvered and outfought the German armor. By the afternoon of the 19th, the German attackers retreated, leaving 50 precious tanks behind. From September 20 to the 25, the commander of the Fifth Panzer Army continued to feed his tank units into a

On the foggy morning of September 19, a panzer brigade with 42 Panther tanks, supported by a regiment of panzer grenadiers, ran into a small section of 4th Armored Division M-4 Sherman tanks. The two American tanks got the first shots in, and destroyed three of the Panther tanks. American tank destroyers quickly joined the battle and destroyed seven more Panther tanks. Pictured is a destroyed Panther tank (model A) that took multiple hits. *Patton Museum*

series of attacks against the Arracourt position. Each assault followed the pattern set on September 19. The German tanks attacked under the cover of morning fog, only to fall back, disorganized by the highly mobile defensive tactics of the 4th Armored Division. The Americans would then launch armored counterattacks in company or battalion strength to rout the German attackers. Wood reinforced his forces around Arracourt with additional tank, infantry, and cavalry elements, and, whenever the weather permitted, aircraft of the XIX TAC added to the growing collection of smoking panzer hulks. On September 29, the German Fifth Panzer Army, with only 25 tanks left, gave up the fight and retreated. The next day, the Americans made a final tank sweep of the area

around Arracourt, thereby ending the Lorraine tank battles.

In the defensive actions fought around Arracourt, the 4th Armored Division claimed 281 German tanks were destroyed. In addition to the losses in tanks, 3,000 Germans died in battle, with another 3,000 taken prisoner. The 4th Armored Division sustained only 626 casualties in all, but the pressure of two continuous months in combat gradually rendered the division ineffective. On October 12, the division pulled out of the line for a month of rest and refitting. The division returned to the fighting in Lorraine in November. By that time, the Lorraine Campaign had evolved into a brutal war of attrition mired down in mud and bloodshed.

By the end of the day, the Germans had lost 43 Panther tanks. The Americans lost only three tank destroyers and five M-4 Sherman tanks. Surprised by their painful encounter with the 4th Armored Division, the tankers of the German panzer brigade tried to turn away on the morning of September 19, to no avail. The 4th Armored Division continued to attack them with everything it had in its inventory. Pictured is an American soldier posing next to a destroyed Panther tank (model A). *National Archives*

Other German armored units, advancing against the 4th Armored Division on September 19, also met with little success. Despite their first day setbacks, the Germans continued their counterattack against Patton's Third Army. On the morning of September 22, the thick fog that had protected the Germans from American fighter-bombers lifted. The P-47s of the XIX TAC quickly appeared overhead and began strafing and bombing runs. Pictured is an American P-47 that was forced to crash-land on a French road. *National Archives*

At the same time the 4th Armored Division was dealing with the Fifth Panzer Army, the 35th Infantry Division faced a series of strong counterattacks by other units of the German Army. The German attacks were beaten off by the division without help on September 27 and 28. In one last major attack, the Germans managed to punch holes in the division's front lines. Extremely worried, Eddy called a meeting of the 35th Infantry Division staff that afternoon. Also present at the meeting was General Gaffey, the Third Army's Chief of Staff, as well as General Grow, whose 6th Armored Division now formed the Third Army reserve. The XII Corps commander, in tacit agreement with the other officers, decided to order a withdrawal of the hard-pressed 35th Infantry Division behind the Seille River. The 6th Armored Division got the job of covering the withdrawal.

Patton, alerted to the meeting by Gaffey, flew to the XII Corps headquarters in Nancy on the same day. On his arrival, Patton quickly countermanded the withdrawal order of the 35th Infantry Division. Instead, he told Eddy, "Counterattack with the 6th Armored. . . . Tell them [the 35th Infantry Division] to hang on." Patton then went on to the 6th Armored Division headquarters east of Nancy, where plans began for the division to attack the next morning. By the end of the day, on October 1, the 6th Armored Division had inflicted heavy casualties on the German forces and pushed them back to their original positions. Americans and Germans then settled down for a long period of

The back of the German counterattack, aimed at Patton's Third Army, finally broke on September 29. The Germans lost close to 300 tanks and suffered 6,000 casualties during the Lorraine tank battles. The Germans were forced to go on the defensive for the rest of the Lorraine Campaign. Pictured are Waffen SS infantrymen who lost their lives in battle with Patton's Third Army. *National Archives*

Patton once stated, "I don't have to tell you who won the war, you know our artillery did." This was a pretty powerful statement from somebody like Patton who is so strongly associated with armored warfare. German prisoners often stated that American artillery fire was extremely effective. Pictured in France is an American artilleryman ready to shove a round into the breach of a 105-mm howitzer M-3. *National Archives*

watchful waiting, beginning a lull in this area that would continue until November.

The Advance of the XX Corps

On the last day of August, tanks of the 7th Armored Division raced across the Meuse River on an intact bridge in the city of Verdun. The crossing at Verdun was close to the last step in a rapid 400-mile advance that the XX Corps had made since August 6. The 5th Infantry Division followed the 7th Armored Division across the Meuse River. At this point, the advance stalled five days for lack of fuel. On September 5, the refueled XX Corps once again began its eastward advance, leading with its mechanized cavalry group.

The general plan involved bypassing Metz with the 7th Armored Division and striking straight for the Saar River and its bridges. The corps' two infantry divisions received the job of capturing the fortified cities of Thionville and Metz. The intricate fortifications of Metz extended many miles around the city on either side of the Moselle River.

Prior to September 5, Major General Walker had little information on the strength and disposition of the German forces along the Moselle River or the fortified positions guarding the respective cities. Early messages from the corps' mechanized cavalry group showed that the Germans were withdrawing. By the night of September 5, new information reached Walker indicating that the Germans were going to defend both Thionville and Metz. Despite this news, the XX Corps staff believed that the

During World War II, American artillery was primarily employed for indirect fire missions. For the gunners to accurately hit targets they could not see, they depended on Forward Observers (FO) at the divisional level for 65 to 75 percent of their targets. FO often had to place themselves in the most exposed positions to see enemy targets. Pictured on top of a French church are two American FO spying on German positions. At corps level (heavy artillery), FO used small artillery observation aircraft, flash detection, or sound ranging equipment. *National Archives*

An American infantry battalion fighting in Europe could have as many as 12 forward observer parties. The FO reported to a battalion liaison officer by radio or telephone. The job of the battalion liaison officers was to control and coordinate the information from his various FO and then pass it on to a Fire Direction Center (FDC). Pictured in France is the radio-equipped jeep of a battalion liaison officer. The soldier on the left is taking information from FO and passing it to the battalion liaison officer (captain) who is double-checking his map. *National Archives*

The battalion liaison officer would then pass on the map coordinates of enemy targets to a Fire Direction Center (FDC). Officers at the FDC would then mass the fire of various artillery batteries on the desired targets. Pictured somewhere in France is an artillery FDC, with enlisted personnel putting a fire plan together on their maps. The soldier on the right of the picture is passing radio information from battalion liaison officers to the two sergeants preparing the firing mission. *National Archives*

Smaller than the 8-inch gun M-1 was the towed 8-inch howitzer M-1, which first entered service in 1942. A little over 1,000 of the howitzers were built. It used the same carriage and breech mechanism as the 155-mm gun M-1, weighed 14 tons, and fired a 200-pound shell out to 18,500 yards. The 8-inch howitzer M-1 was the mainstay of the American Army's heavy artillery units in World War II. Pictured is an 8-inch howitzer M-1 being towed into action by an 18-ton high-speed tractor M-4. *National Archives*

fortified defenses around Thionville and Metz were obsolete and the Germans might not be willing to risk defending them.

Contrary to American intelligence estimates, Hitler had no intention of allowing his forces to abandon the Metz-Thionville defenses. Neither would the German defenders on the west bank of the Moselle River be allowed to withdraw. To defend the Metz-Thionville area from the advancing XX Corps, Hitler had roughly four and a half understrength divisions.

On the night of September 7, Walker launched his main attack toward the Moselle River and the northwest ring of forts that guarded Metz. The Germans had taken the time between August 31 and September 6 to prepare themselves for the attack. From their concrete

fortifications, most of which lay below ground, the Germans rained down antitank and artillery fire on the advancing American soldiers. Despite heavy losses, the corps pressed its attacks until September 14. Fighter-bombers and heavy artillery failed to reduce the concrete emplacements, and the German soldiers defending the area counterattacked any attempt to get near the defense positions. Americans occupied positions 1,000 yards from the first line of German forts, when on corps orders, the main effort aimed to the south of Metz.

The XX Corps River Crossings

The southern advance toward Metz that began on September 7 also ran into fierce German resistance. Unwilling to halt their attack,

American soldiers reached the Moselle River near the town of Dornot on that same evening. The next morning, they attempted a river assault, supported by corps artillery, to the east side, but the Germans counterattacked with a ferocity and determination that astounded the American defenders. In addition, the Germans pounded the bridgehead area with artillery fire. With losses mounting, the last American assault troops withdrew on September 11 under the protective fire of corps artillery.

On the morning of September 10, while the Germans were busy concentrating their forces on repelling the XX Corps bridgehead at Dornot, Walker ordered another bridgehead at a point 4,000 yards south near Arnaville. The Germans quickly recovered from their initial surprise and launched the expected counterat-tacks. From across the river, the XX Corps now had 13 artillery battalions firing in support of the Arnaville bridgehead. The few German tanks that managed to get through the curtain of American artillery fire were driven off by bazooka fire.

On September 11, the corps engineers prepared a ford north of Arnaville, and tanks and tank destroyers rushed across the river into the bridgehead zone. By the afternoon of the 12th, the corps engineers completed a large bridge across the Moselle. By quickly rushing additional forces into the Arnaville bridgehead, the XX Corps managed to repel all further German counterattacks, the largest of which began on September 17 and was only stopped at the last moment by furious hand-to-hand fighting.

By securing the bridgehead at Arnaville and

Due to a shortage of heavy artillery-towing vehicles (both wheeled and tracked) in Europe, many large artillery pieces were towed by tanks or tank destroyers (with their guns and turrets removed). Pictured is a turretless M-10A1 tank destroyer towing an 8-inch M-1. In this configuration the M-10A1 was redesignated as an M-35 Prime Moving towing vehicle. In its role as a towing vehicle, the M-35 had a six-man crew and was fitted with an air compressor (for the artillery carriage air brakes) and towing pintle. *National Archives*

In mid-July 1944, Eisenhower had asked for a plan that could employ the First Allied Airborne Army in putting a bridgehead across the Rhine. This plan eventually developed into Operation Market-Garden (September 17 through 26). This badly planned operation quickly turned into disaster, with heavy losses to the Allied airborne forces. Despite the failure of Operation Market-Garden, Eisenhower, under constant pressure from Montgomery, continued to devote the majority of the Allied logistical support system to the northern advance of Montgomery's 21st Army Group. On September 25, Bradley was forced to order Patton's Third Army to go on the defensive. Pictured is an American soldier examining a gouge inflicted by a German high-velocity antitank round in the lower front hull armor of a destroyed M-4 Sherman tank. *National Archives*

capturing Thionville, the XX Corps managed to partially outflank several of the major fortresses on the western side of the Moselle River. In response to the initial success, Hitler ordered his First Army on September 16 to reinforce the areas on either side of Metz to prevent the XX Corps from encircling the city. On the same day, the 7th Armored Division and the 5th Infantry Division began an attack aimed at crossing both the Seille and Nied Rivers. The ultimate goal was to reach the rear of Metz. Against heavy German resistance, nobody made much headway.

The two divisions restarted their advance to the Seille River on September 18. By the afternoon of September 20, they reached the river after stiff fighting. Two early attempts at crossing the river the next day failed. The 7th Armored Division began making plans for a major crossing of the river on the night of September 23, but it was never made because that afternoon General Bradley ordered the division to be transferred to First Army control. The division quickly received orders to move north to its new location in Belgium. This move made it necessary for the 5th Infantry Division to

Even though the Third Army was officially on the defensive, beginning on September 25, Patton kept up a number of local offensive operations. Most of these operations were aimed at breaking through the ring of old forts that protected the French fortress city of Metz. Pictured is an American 155-mm howitzer M1 at the moment of firing. The barrel is in full recoil. To increase the firing elevation of their weapon, the gun-crew members have dug their howitzer into the ground. *National Archives*

discontinue its advance toward the rear of Metz and go on the defensive, forcing it to give up some of the ground it had fought so hard to capture.

On September 25, Bradley sent a message to Eisenhower telling him that he had ordered Patton to go on the defensive with the entire Third Army. At the same time, Bradley also informed Eisenhower that he had given Patton permission to make some minor adjustments in his present lines. Patton used this vague order from Bradley to continue attacking the German positions throughout the Third Army sector, despite serious shortages of everything from gasoline to ammunition.

Fort Busting

On September 27, Walker ordered the 5th Infantry Division to assault Fort Driant, five miles southwest of Metz. The powerful old fort with its batteries of huge guns was a thorn in the side of the XX Corps. From its commanding heights, the Germans controlled the approach to Metz along the Moselle Valley. To Walker, the capture of the fort was essential before a successful advance up the Moselle Valley would work. The assault on the fort began with both air and artillery support. As the assault troops began to approach the fort, they met interlacing bands of machine-gun fire along a huge moat 20 yards wide and 30 feet deep. The concrete walls of the fort were 7 feet thick with barbed wire rolls up to 20 feet deep covering every approach. On top of the fort lay revolving gun turrets protected by thick steel armor. Against such defenses the assault troops of the 5th Infantry Division stood little chance of success and pulled out as fast as possible.

Unfavorable weather postponed further attacks against Fort Driant. American officers reviewed lessons learned from the first attack and developed a more ambitious plan for the second assault. On October 3, planes of the XIX TAC dropped napalm on the fort. At the same time, a combined force of tanks, infantry, and

One of the initial objectives of Patton's XX Corps was the reduction of Fort Driant, which formed a part of the outer ring of Metz fortresses. It held an important height from which it could direct the artillery fire from other forts on approaching American forces. Built in 1902, Fort Driant was the most modern and the strongest fort in the German defensive system. Pictured is Major General Walton H. Walker (on the left), commander of the XX Corps, viewing a terrain model of Fort Driant. The officer in the center of the picture is Major General Leroy S. Irwin, commander of the 5th Infantry Division, whose men were tasked with capturing Fort Driant. To the right of the picture is General George S. Marshall. Walker's XX Corps was ill-prepared for its first major assault on Fort Driant. His troops were tired, and there were serious shortages of fuel, ammunition, and reinforcements. *Patton Museum*

engineers carrying everything from flame-throwers to bangalore torpedoes attacked the fort from the north and south. The southern force succeeded in penetrating the walls on the first day of the attack. Once inside the many underground passages of Fort Driant, there began a strange, confusing fight that came to be known as the "battle of the tunnels."

Within a week's time, the American soldiers inside the German fort had had enough. Patton commented, "If we could get the supplies we need and with three good days of weather, we could take it." He went on to say, "In fact, I am not going to let these soldiers get killed until we have something on our side." On the morning of October 10, Major Generals Gaffey, Walker, and various divisional commanders decided

Right: Fort Driant, like many of the other Metz forts, was a massive structure made of concrete, bricks, and steel. The concrete walls on some of the Metz forts were several feet thick. The various casemates that made up the individual forts were built to be flush with the ground. Only some armored observation posts and pillboxes lay above the surface. Fort Driant was surrounded by a dry moat, 20 feet wide and up to 30 feet deep in some places. To prevent infantry from getting too close, barbed wire to a depth of 60 feet encircled the entire fort. All the various structures that made up the fort were connected by underground concrete-lined tunnels. Finally, the Germans had taken the time to provide the defenders with adequate water, storage space for food, and ammunition. Pictured are American soldiers looking over a massive concrete pillbox (with dry moat) recently captured from its German defenders. *National Archives*

Army Air Force P-47 fighter-bombers led the assault on Fort Driant on the morning of September 27 by dropping 1,000-pound bombs and napalm on the fort, with negligible results. American self-propelled artillery pieces, like the 155-mm gun M-12 pictured here, firing at point-blank range, also had no effect on the German defensive positions. *Real War Photos*

Despite American troops' best efforts, the assault on Fort Driant, launched on September 27, failed. A second assault on the fort began on October 3. In the initial stages of the second assault on Fort Driant, some American soldiers made it into the fort. Due to fierce German resistance, however, they had to be pulled out, with heavy losses, on the nights of October 12 and 13. The failure to capture the fort represented the first publicized reverse suffered by Patton's Third Army. Pictured is a heavily damaged German steel observation post, common to many of the German-held Metz forts. *National Archives*

that sufficient forces were not available to complete the capture of Fort Driant. By the morning of October 14, all remaining American soldiers inside the fort withdrew. Losses for the assault on Fort Driant cost the 5th Infantry Division over 500 men.

Plans for a New Offensive

Eisenhower's general policy throughout the campaign in Europe was to keep constant pressure on the German ground forces all along their lines. In the middle of October, Eisenhower began thinking about giving the American armies a larger role in the Allied advance to the Rhine. On October 17, Eisenhower visited Patton to talk about restarting the Third Army's advance. The next day, Eisenhower met with Bradley and Montgomery in Belgium to make plans for a new southern advance to the Rhine by both the American First and Ninth Armies. The Ninth Army, under the command of Lieutenant General Alan Simpson, came up

With the failure to capture Fort Driant, the Third Army began a lengthy period of time in which little or no combat operations took place. Instead, Patton concentrated on reinforcing and rebuilding the Third Army for its next offensive operation. Pictured is Patton and Major General John Millikin, the III Corps commander, looking over aerial reconnaissance maps of German positions on the floor of Patton's headquarters. Bradley assigned the III Corps to Patton's Third Army on October 19. *Patton Museum*

from Brittany at the end of September and took over the northern sector of the First Army's front. Eisenhower's plan called for the American southern advance to the Rhine to be held in conjunction with the northern advance to the Rhine by Montgomery's 21st Army Group. In Eisenhower's original plan, the Third Army was to play only a secondary role by advancing in a northeasterly direction in support of the First and Ninth Armies' main advance to the Rhine.

On October 19, Patton wrote a personal letter to Bradley setting forth his plans for a Third Army drive up to the West Wall that would take three days at the most. Patton also assured Bradley that the Germans facing his forces had all their strength in their front lines. Once they overran the German front lines, the Third Army stood a good chance of breaking through the West Wall and driving rapidly to the Rhine.

On October 22, Bradley issued an order that stated, "12th Army Group will regroup and prepare for an advance by all three Armies to the Rhine River." Bradley told Patton at the same time that, "If all the armies . . . attacked simultaneously, it might end the war." The actual launching of the American southern advance would depend on a number of factors, the most important being the availability of adequate supplies. Another factor almost as important was the weather. Without decent weather, the XIX TAC could not provide air support for the planned American advance. Within these parameters, Eisenhower figured the combined advance of all his armies could begin sometime between November 1 and 5.

By the end of the first week in November, the required supplies for an advance to the Rhine River began appearing in Bradley's 12th Army Group sector. At the same time, it became apparent that strong German resistance in the north would delay the advance of Montgomery's 21st Army Group. On November 2,

Bradley visited Patton's headquarters to inform him that neither the British nor the other American armies were ready to begin the planned advance. Bradley therefore asked if the Third Army could begin the offensive by itself. Patton promptly answered that the Third Army would be able to attack on 24-hour notice. Patton's staff had begun the planning for such an operation as early as September. Patton informed his commander that the Third Army should begin the offensive when the weather permitted the air forces to begin softening up the German defensive positions.

The Third Army received two orders from the 12th Army Group on November 3 for its planned objectives. First, it was to encircle Metz

During the Third Army's October lull in operations, Patton spent a lot of time trying to convince Eisenhower and Bradley to use his army for a new advance to the Rhine River. Unknown to Patton, Eisenhower had already begun formulating plans for new offensive operations to begin in November. Unfortunately, Eisenhower decided that Patton's Third Army was to play only a secondary role in the upcoming operations. Pictured is Patton at an ordnance branch display of a new tank-mounted flamethrower, near the fighting front in France. *Patton Museum*

On November 2, Bradley told Patton that the other Allied armies were unable to begin offensive operations. Bradley asked Patton if his Third Army was ready to begin operations. Patton answered Bradley's question by telling him that the Third Army could be on the move in 24 hours. As before, the main goal of this new offensive operation was the capture of Metz and an advance toward Germany. Pictured on the outskirts of Metz is an American M-10 tank destroyer dug into a hull-down defensive position. *Real War Photos*

from both the north and south and destroy any German forces trying to withdraw from the area. Second, it was to capture the German cities of Mainz, Frankfurt, and Darmstadt. If these two goals were successfully met, the Third

Army was to prepare itself for a deeper advance into Germany.

On the morning of November 4, Patton addressed his Third Army headquarters' staff, "Gentlemen, Third Army has been given the

Due to poor weather conditions, Patton's planned offensive had to be delayed until November 8. The attack would be launched from the Nancy area, with three infantry divisions leading it. Behind the infantry division, two armored divisions would stand ready to exploit any breakthrough of the German defensive lines. Pictured is an American M-4A1 Sherman tank armed with a 76-mm gun. To increase the ability of American tanks to cross soft or muddy ground, many were fitted with track extensions, called "duckbills," as seen in this picture. *National Archives*

great honor of leading the new offensive in the west. Our D-Day, as you know, is any time from tomorrow until the 8th depending on the weather. Despite the difficulties we face, and notwithstanding my considerable talents as a bull artist, I can assure you that we will succeed

in breaking through the Siegfried Line, penetrate into the heart of Germany, and win the war. I want hard-hitting and unremitting effort pressing our plan of operations. And always keep in mind that the Rhine is our objective. As a result of my intimate relations with God," he

Besides the M-7 self-propelled 105-mm howitzer, many American armored divisions employed the M-8 self-propelled 75-mm howitzer to support medium tank battalions. The four-man crew of the M-8 pictured here is preparing for its next fire mission by cleaning the barrel of its weapon and loading up with additional ammunition. The M-8 was based on the chassis of the M-5 light tank series, with the howitzer mounted in an open-topped turret. Cadillac built 1,778 examples of the M-8 between September 1942 and January 1944. *National Archives*

concluded, "I am in a position to express complete assurance that we will have the good weather we need for a lucky jump-off."

On the eve of the November offensive, Patton's resupplied and reinforced Third Army consisted of three armored divisions: the 4th, 6th, and the 10th. It also had six infantry divisions: the 5th, 26th, 80th, 83rd, 90th, and the 95th. There were also a large number of nondivisional units attached to the Third Army. These included five tank battalions and 14 tank destroyer battalions, most of which were assigned to the five infantry divisions. Six mechanized cavalry reconnaissance squadrons would provide the eyes and ears of the Third

Army during the upcoming advance.

To provide battlefield support, 38 field artillery battalions, a total of almost 700 guns, were provided. In total, Patton's Third Army consisted of a quarter of a million men when the offensive began on November 8. Protection for the Third Army from any Luftwaffe attacks came from 22 attached antiaircraft battalions.

Still facing the Third Army on November 8 was the German First Army of roughly 87,000 men divided into nine divisions with about 100 tanks and self-propelled guns. There was a single panzer division, one panzer grenadier division, and several new volksgrenadier (infantry) divisions of 10,000 men each. In addition to the nine divisions, the First Army also controlled a large number of independent fortress, security, antiaircraft, and machine gun units, most of which fought out of the numerous Metz forts.

The November Advance

Despite Patton's professed connection with the Almighty, it rained almost constantly in the Lorraine during the first week of November. On November 7, two high-ranking officers visited Patton to ask that he postpone the attack due to the poor weather conditions. Patton replied, "The attack will go on, rain or no rain and I'm sure it will succeed." Patton then stated, "I think you better recommend the men you would like appointed as your successors." Both officers quickly ended their protests and went back to their respective headquarters.

Patton began his main advance to the Rhine River on November 8, with the XII Corps

The M-7 and M-8 howitzers proved to be unpopular with their American crews due to the lack of overhead armored protection. A replacement arrived in the form of a Sherman tank, armed with a 105-mm howitzer, mounted in a fully enclosed armored turret. Beginning in February 1943, Chrysler built almost 5,000 of the 105-mm howitzer-equipped Shermans. The majority of howitzer-equipped Shermans were built on the M-4A3 series of Sherman tanks as pictured. *National Archives*

American infantry units often depended on mortars for close-range fire support missions. Infantrymen often refer to their mortars as pocket artillery. The largest mortar in the American Army inventory to see widespread use in Europe was the 4.2-inch chemical mortar. Weighing in at 330 pounds, the 4.2-inch mortar fired a large 32-pound high explosive round up to 4,500 yards. A well-trained mortar crew could fire up to 20 rounds per minute for short periods. *National Archives*

During the initial stages of Patton's November 8 assault across the flooded Seille River, some limited progress was achieved. The big breakthrough of the German lines envisioned by Patton, however, failed to materialize. Contributing to the lack of American success was the constant rain that turned parts of the Lorraine area into a swampy mess. A limited road net and stiff German resistance also made progress difficult. Pictured is an American M-4A1 Sherman tank (armed with a 76-mm gun) that was hit by German antitank fire and caught fire. Notice the long wooden logs fitted on the side of the hull for added protection. *National Archives*

attacking on a 30-mile front. It started with an early morning artillery barrage that lasted three and a half hours. After lifting the barrage, the XII Corps sent the 26th, 35th, and 80th Infantry Divisions forward.

The goal of the three infantry divisions was to cross the flooded Seille River and provide maneuver room for armored divisions to exploit any holes punched in the German lines by the infantry divisions. The three infantry divisions achieved some initial success against the surprised German defenders, but not the maneuver room needed for the armored divi-

sions. Eddy ordered his two armored divisions across the Seille anyway. Once on the eastern side of the Seille, the armored divisions found their progress stalled by both mud and German minefields. In eight days of fierce fighting, the various divisions of the XII Corps gained only 15 miles. The German Army Group commander had easily anticipated both the place and date of Patton's attack and planned his defenses accordingly.

Unlike Operation Cobra, during which the German lines collapsed after some brief fighting, the German resistance in the Lorraine

On November 9, Patton's XX Corps launched itself in an advance aimed at capturing Metz. Despite poor weather conditions and tough German resistance, two divisions of the XX Corps linked up behind Metz on November 19, cutting off the German defenders from any further reinforcements or supplies. The city fell to the men of the XX Corps on November 22. Pictured here are American soldiers in Metz, looking door to door for German snipers. *National Archives*

(aided by the heavy autumn rains) grew in strength and intensity as time progressed, adding to the Third Army's toll of casualties and lost equipment. Compounding the problems of rain and mud, it snowed on the second day of Patton's advance. Bitter cold weather added to the misery of Patton's troops.

The XII Corps' left flank stood guarded by the XX Corps, whose general advance began on November 9. The XX Corps, with three infantry divisions and a single armored division, had the job of surrounding and capturing Metz. Inside the city were roughly 14,000 German troops, of

which about 10,000 were combat troops. After securing Metz, the XX Corps was to drive northeastward toward the Saar between the German cities of Saarburg and Saarlautern. This area was referred to as the Saar-Moselle Triangle. If the XX Corps could successfully seize this area, it could then continue its advance toward the Rhine in a northeasterly direction.

The XX corps began its advance on Metz with an attack by the 90th and 5th Infantry Divisions on either side of the city. The 90th Infantry Division crossed the Moselle River north of Metz and the 5th Infantry Division crossed the Seille River to the south. Their job was to encircle Metz. The northern advance was assisted by the 10th Armored Division, com-

manded by Major General W. H. H. Morris. At the same time the 10th was assisting in the encirclement, it was to send armored reconnais-

Even though Patton's XX Corps took control of the city of Metz on November 22, many of the forts surrounding Metz continued to fight on till the bloody end. Rather than attempt to capture the forts with more costly infantry assaults, the men of the XX Corps decided to wait the Germans out. As their supplies ran out and their morale plummeted, the Germans in the various remaining forts decided to surrender. Fort Driant surrendered on December 8. The last German-held Metz fort surrendered on December 13. Pictured are American soldiers taking the surrender of the last Metz fort. *Real War Photos*

In the closing days of November, Patton's Third Army cleared out most of the German forces along the eastern bank of the Saar River. Elements of the XII Corps managed to establish two bridgeheads across the Saar River on November 23. Despite some limited success in the November offensive operations, Patton's Third Army had not penetrated the German West Wall or gotten much closer to the Rhine River. Pictured is Patton conferring with Major General Horace L. McBride, commander of the 80th Infantry Division. *Patton Museum*

One of the biggest problems for Patton's Third Army in the Lorraine Campaign was the weather. The climate of the Lorraine tends to extremes of heat and cold, precipitation and dryness. Due to the westerly winds in the area, the Lorraine normally receives two or three times as much rain as areas of France just to the west. In the autumn and winter of 1944, the rain that fell was two to three times the amount usually recorded; in November 1944 alone, 6.95 inches of rain fell. Pictured are American soldiers trying to dig foxholes in the mud of France. *Real War Photos*

sance columns east toward the Saar River to look for bridging sites. The 95th Infantry Division had the job of containing the German forces west of the Moselle. At an indicated time, the 95th Division would drive in the German

forces west of the Moselle River, cross the river, and capture Metz.

Unfortunately, the advance was plagued by the same problems of poor weather and stiff German resistance as had been faced by the XII

An American soldier armed with an M-1 Thompson submachine gun carefully looks over his surroundings. The M-1 version of the Thompson was standardized by the army in April 1942. A later version was known as the M-1A1. Both versions weighed a little over 10 pounds, and fired a .45-caliber slug, from either a 20- or 30-round box magazine. The Thompson was a difficult and expensive weapon to build, but was well liked by the troops because of its reliability.
National Archives

Corps. It was not until November 19 that the 5th and 90th infantry divisions finally linked up behind Metz. Most of the Germans in the city lost the will to fight on and began surrendering in large numbers. The city officially fell into American hands on November 22. An unhappy Patton wrote: "I had hoped to win this battle by 11 November, as it was my birthday and my lucky day in West Africa [Patton was referring to his landing in North Africa two years before]. However, I did not win it."

With his troops exhausted, Patton soon abandoned any hope of a quick breakthrough to the Rhine. He had to remain content with simply driving the Third Army steadily forward. Patton would write: "The impetus of the attack is naturally slacking due to the fatigue of the men." At the end of November, some units of the Third Army managed to push within sight of the Saar but did not cross the river. Within the XX Corps area of operations, the Saar River flowed through Germany. In the XII Corps area, on the other hand, most of the Saar River flowed through France. The inability of Patton's Third Army to achieve a breakthrough of the German lines was matched by the lack of

A squad of American infantrymen enter a ruined French town looking for German snipers. The soldier in the foreground is carrying a Browning .30-caliber M-1919A4 light machine gun. The A-4 version of the Browning weighed about 32 pounds and had a rate of fire of between 400 to 450 rounds per minute. The A4 Browning was normally fired from a metal tripod. *National Archives*

success of both the American First and Ninth armies.

The only American military force to reach the Rhine River during the November advance was the 6th Army Group, south of the Third Army. The 6th Army Group, led by General Jacob L. Devers, consisted of the American Seventh Army and the First Free French Army. The 6th Army Group landed on the Mediterranean coast of southern France on August 15, and advanced northeast to the German border, where it joined ranks with Bradley's 12th Army Group on September 12. On November 27, Eisenhower, acting upon a suggestion from Patton, ordered Devers to attack northward with the two American corps. Their objective was to breach the West Wall, thereby aiding Patton's Third Army in its drive toward the Saar River. Eisenhower wanted the 6th Army Group's advance to attract German divisions away from

other areas, making it easier for the other Allied armies to advance.

The Germans failed to fall for Eisenhower's ploy and withdrew only a single infantry division from north of the Third Army's sector. Despite the help from the 6th Army Group, Patton's Third Army still made little headway. On December 4, Eisenhower wrote to Marshall that the Germans "should be able to maintain a strong defensive front for some time, assisted by weather, floods and muddy ground."

Eisenhower's biggest concern was his inability to get the Germans to commit their newly refitted armored divisions. He knew from Magic/Ultra reports that the Germans had amassed eight to nine armored divisions in their strategic reserve. He was also aware, as early as November 1, of German plans for a large counterattack on the Western Front. For many different reasons, this information was

On December 4, the XX Corps managed to capture a bridge across the Saar River and began attacking the German West Wall fortifications located on the eastern bank of the river. By December 6, the XX Corps put two additional bridgeheads across the Saar River. Pictured are American 2 1/2 ton 6x6 trucks bringing up bridging equipment (pontoons) for a river-crossing operation. The section of the West Wall attacked by Patton's XX Corps was considered by the Germans to be the strongest in the entire West Wall system. *National Archives*

not taken seriously by Eisenhower or the SHAEF staff. In what would prove to be a massive failure of American intelligence work, the Germans managed to surprise the Allies on December 16, with their last great offensive action of the war. They launched 41 divisions and 1,500 tanks against four American divisions stationed in Belgium and Luxembourg. This German offensive would go down in history as The Battle of the Bulge.

On the morning of November 23, the first elements of the XII Corps crossed the Saar River (in France) north of Sarrebourg in two locations. By the end of the month, the XII Corps had cleared almost all of the remaining German positions from the west bank of the Saar. On November 24, advance elements of the XX Corps reached the Saar River in Germany. As the bulk of the XX Corps approached the Saar, the Germans resisted savagely for every foot of ground. The main goal of the XX Corps was to seize the heavily defended German industrial center of Saarlautern and its vital bridges across the Saar River, where the West Wall paralleled the eastern bank of the Saar River.

December Operations

In a surprise attack on December 4, elements of the XX Corps captured one of the bridges across the Saar River. The corps rushed troops, tanks, and tank destroyers across the bridge as quickly as possible, despite strong German counterattacks. Patton wrote, "We are attacking the Siegfried Line. I know that there are many generals with my reputation who would not have dared to do so because 'they are more afraid of losing a battle than anxious to win one.' I do not believe that any of these lines are impregnable. If we get through, we will materially shorten the war. There is no if about getting through; I am sure we will!"

By December 6, the XX Corps had two more bridgeheads across the Saar River. The fighting along the West Wall soon developed into a bitter slugging match against tenacious German resistance. Adding to the difficulty was a constant cold rain that prevented Patton's troops from receiving any air support. On December 3, Patton wrote in his diary, "I have never seen or imagined such a hell hole of a country. There is about four inches of liquid mud over everything, and it rains all the time, not hard but steadily."

Patton's troops had to attack German pillboxes that were placed to support each other and lay down a continuous band of fire along

The crossing of the Saar River caused serious concern at all of the German higher headquarters. The Germans quickly rushed in any units they had in an attempt to destroy the Third Army bridgeheads across the Saar River. The American soldiers were hampered by poor weather conditions that prevented the air support they needed. Between December 1 until the Lorraine Campaign ended, the XIX TAC had only six days suitable for full-scale operations. Pictured are American infantrymen passing through part of the West Wall defenses. *National Archives*

On December 16, the Germans launched a massive counterattack against American forces in the Ardennes. The aim of the German counterattack was to split the Allied armies in half and recapture the important Belgian port of Antwerp. In response to this major threat, Patton's Third Army ended its Lorraine Campaign on December 20, and turned northward to attack the German forces in what would become better known to most as "The Battle of the Bulge." Pictured is a German Tiger II tank carrying paratroopers into battle against the Americans in the Ardennes. The Ardennes is a heavily wooded and hilly area located in Luxembourg and Belgium. *National Archives*

all likely approaches. When XX Corps soldiers managed to fight their way close to the enemy's defenses, the Germans retreated into their pillboxes and called artillery on their own positions. Most of the German pillboxes were dug in flush with the ground with only a gun turret exposed. In addition, they were carefully camouflaged with natural growth, and were hard to locate even from the air. Even when they *were* detected, the larger pillboxes were hard to destroy. Artillery alone was rarely sufficient. One steel turret along the defenses withstood several direct hits from a 155-mm self-propelled gun and over 50 rounds of 90-mm fire from an M-36 tank destroyer. In addition to the pillboxes, the American soldiers had to contend with minefields and booby traps.

The XX Corps continued its attempt to breach the West Wall until December 20. By then, the massive German counterattack in the Ardennes had compelled Patton and his Third Army to discontinue their aggressive attacks to the east and to swing the biggest part of their forces to the north. Patton's Lorraine Campaign came to an abrupt and inglorious ending. Without sadness, Patton embarked on a new campaign that would bring both him and his Third Army historic fame.

During Patton's 16-week campaign in Lorraine, the Third Army liberated or conquered approximately 5,000 square miles of enemy-held territory. The Germans lost three highly important defensive positions, the Moselle, the Nied, and the Saar Rivers. Also lost to the Ger-

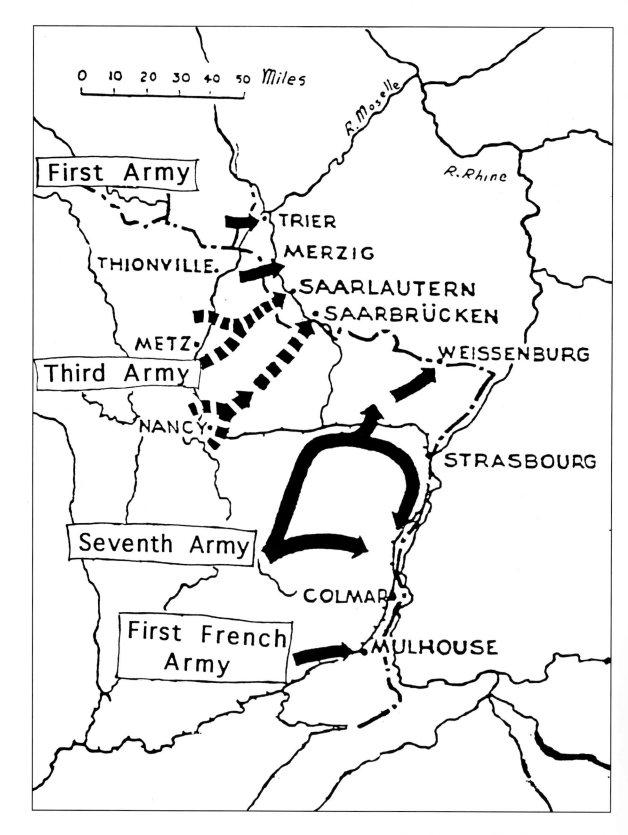

man war economy were the important iron ore mines located in the Lorraine as well as some in the Saar Basin. The West Wall, however, remained intact and blocked the American advance to the Rhine. An official postwar study of Patton's Lorraine Campaign stated, "Patton failed to concentrate Third Army's resources of the corps engaged in decisive operations. . . .

The Lorraine Campaign cost Patton's Third Army 105 light tanks and 298 medium tanks. The tank losses suffered by the German panzer units in the September battles had been much higher than those inflicted on the American armored units. In November and December, however, American tank losses incurred in the slow advance through the Lorraine mud probably were considerably higher than those of the Germans. Pictured is an American M-4 Sherman tank that took a high-velocity German antitank round in its hull side. *Patton Museum*

The corps commanders were trapped between Patton, who continually urged aggressive action, and the grim realities of terrain, weather, and a determined enemy . . . [and] at times became preoccupied with local problems and lost sight of the broader issues," resulting in little cooperation among the corps and a consequently disjointed campaign.

During the Lorraine Campaign, the Third Army suffered 6,657 killed, 36,406 wounded, and 12,119 missing in action. In addition, the Third Army lost another 42,088 men to so-called "non-battle" casualties. These were men evacuated because of fatigue, exposure, and disease. German casualties during the Lorraine Campaign are much harder to determine. Records show that 75,000 German soldiers passed through Third Army POW cages during the campaign.

CONCLUSION

On December 16, Patton received an important phone call from Bradley telling him that the 10th Armored Division needed to be transferred to the First Army control in the Ardennes that night. Patton, who had planned to employ the 10th Armored Division in his pre-Christmas Saar campaign, protested to no avail.

Patton knew of the German attack in the Ardennes on the morning of December 16, but did not believe that it was a major counterattack at first. On December 18, Bradley called Patton twice, leaving no doubt that the situation faced by the First Army was serious indeed. On December 19, Eisenhower ordered all offensive operations south of the Moselle halted. The Third Army was to turn over all its front-line positions to Devers' 6th Army Group except for elements of the XX Corps on the border of the Saar. When this was accomplished, Patton was to throw the bulk of his forces at the southern flank of the German forces advancing in the Ardennes. Two days later, Patton broke off his battle in the Saar and attacked toward Bastogne. In what Bradley described as, "one of the most astonishing feats of generalship of our campaign in the West," Patton managed to turn the bulk of his Third Army 90 degrees and move it north 50 to 70 miles into a new attack.

The 101st Airborne Division occupied the important road and rail center of Bastogne on December 19, with the support of other units, including the 705th Tank Destroyer Battalion. The next day, advancing German units surrounded Bastogne. On the afternoon of December 21, Patton launched an effort to relieve Bastogne. Major General John Millikin's III Corps, consisting of the 4th Armored Division (now commanded by Major General Hugh J. Gaffey) and the 26th and 80th Infantry Divisions, struck at the southern flank of the German breakthrough in the Luxembourg section of the Ardennes. The III Corps' advance was followed with an advance by the divisions of the XII and XX Corps. By December 26, the first tanks of the 4th Armored Division reached the town, but due to stiff German resistance, Bastogne was not truly secure until January 7. By that time, the German winter offensive had died in the bleak, snow-covered fields of Belgium. Harassed on the ground and from the air, the Germans began pulling back their badly mauled armies.

By January 28, 1945, all the ground that the Allies had lost to the Germans in the Ardennes counterattack had been retaken. The Germans lost almost 100,000 men of which 24,000 died. In addition, the Germans lost thousands of wheeled and tracked vehicles. Total casualties for the 29 American and four British divisions deployed in the Ardennes numbered almost 77,000 men. Patton's Third Army suffered 35,525 casualties in the Ardennes. Unlike the Allies, the Germans could not replace their losses in men or equipment.

The German counterattack in the Ardennes managed to halt the advance of the Allied armies on the Rhine River, forcing Eisenhower to spend much of December concerned with the elimination of the German forces in the Ardennes. His staff continued working on plans to clear the area west of the Rhine in preparation for crossing the river and for advancing eastward into Germany. At the end of December, Eisenhower decided that the advance of the American armies toward Germany must continue only after the Germans in the Ardennes retreated.

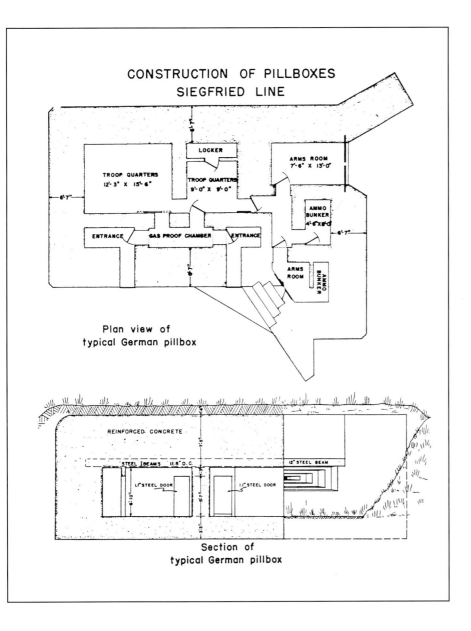

CONSTRUCTION OF PILLBOXES
SIEGFRIED LINE

Plan view of
typical German pillbox

Section of
typical German pillbox

On January 18, Eisenhower directed Bradley to continue his offensive, instructing him "to take advantage of the enemy's present unfavorable position in the Ardennes, inflict the maximum losses on him, seize any opportunity of breaching the Siegfried Line and, if successful, advance northeast on the axis Pruem-Euskirchen." Eisenhower also informed Bradley that if the attacks of the First and Third Armies failed in these objectives, he would order them to go on the defensive at the end of January and pass the attack on to Montgomery's 21st Army Group.

By the end of January, Bradley's forces had pushed the Germans back to the West Wall fortifications in their sector. Bradley's troops were also beginning to encounter delays, and there

appeared little chance of meeting the objectives set by Eisenhower. Bradley showed no surprise when Eisenhower ordered him to go on the defensive on February 1, except for an attack by First Army units to clear the Roer Dam area. Eisenhower also ordered Bradley to divert divisions from both the First and Third Armies to reinforce the Ninth Army for its upcoming attack.

On February 2, Bradley asked Patton and the commander of the First Army if they could continue their advances until February 10 with their remaining divisions. Both army commanders indicated that they would do their best to keep moving forward. Bradley gave tacit permission for Patton to make limited advances in the Eiffel region north of the Moselle river. The

Walking in the footsteps of the man ahead helps conceal the number of men in the patrol.

matter was kept quiet so as not to draw objections from Montgomery. On February 23, the First Army crossed the Roer River and then advanced to the Erft River by February 28. This operation allowed the First Army to protect the right flank of the Ninth Army as it began driving northward.

To the south of the First Army, Patton had never stopped pushing his Third Army slowly forward. By the end of February, the Third Army had opened a path up the Pruem Valley toward the Rhine River, cleared the Moselle-Saar Triangle, and passed through most of the West Wall defenses in its sector to within three miles of the city of Trier. As the Third Army continued to push forward, Patton pleaded with Bradley to give him an additional division so he could mount a large attack in the area of Trier and the Saar. Patton also pointed out that the great majority of American soldiers in Europe were not fighting and warned, "All of us in high position will surely be held accountable for the failure to take offensive action when offensive action is possible."

Bradley did begin a new offensive on March 1 and assigned Patton the job of crossing the Kyll River, located 12 miles inside Germany. The Rhine lay some 50 miles east of the Kyll. Once a bridgehead over the Kyll became secure, Patton's forces were to advance and seize the area located between the German cities of Mainz and Koblenz. If the German defenses in the area were weak, the Third Army was to secure a Moselle bridgehead and clear the enemy from the area, then link up with the First Army.

Patton wasted no time picking up the tempo of the Third Army's advance. Two of Patton's divisions captured Trier and a bridge across the Moselle on the night of March 1. The next morning Patton received a message from Eisenhower's staff telling him to bypass Trier, since it would take four divisions to capture. Patton sent a message back, "Have taken Trier with two divisions. What do you want me to do? Give it back?"

On March 6, the first elements of the Third Army crossed the Kyll River. The next day, elements of both the First and Third Armies met up a few miles short of the Rhine. By the night of March 7, the 4th Armored Division managed to penetrate three miles short of the Rhine near the city of Koblenz. In the process, Patton's tankers had spread havoc throughout the German defenses west of the Rhine River and north of the Moselle River. The 4th Armored Division did not attempt to cross the Rhine. Instead, it headed southward toward the Moselle. On March 8, Eisenhower ordered the Third Army to assist the Seventh Army in its southern offensive in the Saar-Palatinate Triangle. This area contained the last sizable German forces still west of the Rhine river. The Saar-Palatinate area itself lay south of the Moselle river and embraced more than 3,000 square miles. By March 13, Patton had five of his divisions along the Moselle River and another four located northeast of Trier.

Major General Alexander M. Patch began his Seventh Army's advance on March 15, aided by Patton's forces located north of his position. Third Army armored columns soon swept across the rear of the German defenses in the Saar-Palatinate Triangle. On March 21, elements of the Seventh Army linked up with the Third Army. By March 25, the Saar-Palatinate Triangle was overrun, and the Seventh Army began its preparations for a crossing of the Rhine River.

On March 7, elements of the First Army captured a bridge across the Rhine at the town of Remagen. The First Army wasted no time trying to expand its bridgehead on the eastern bank of the Rhine. Despite frantic German counterattacks, the First Army kept enlarging its bridgehead and pushing deeper into Germany. At the same time, Patton's forces were also crossing the Rhine. The Third Army's assault across the Rhine began shortly before midnight on March 22. By the next morning, six battalions of infantry had been put across the river at a cost of only 28 casualties. The Seventh Army first got across the Rhine on March

26. During February and March, the Third Army suffered 25,000 casualties but captured 100,000 German prisoners.

At the same time the Allied armies were crossing the Rhine, the Soviet Army was encircling the German capital of Berlin. This development forced Eisenhower to rule out Berlin as an Allied military objective. Even the capture of the Ruhr became less important to Eisenhower as his intelligence experts informed him that the Germans had been moving important factories out of the area. Despite this, Eisenhower had Montgomery's 21st Army Group and Bradley's First Army advance on the Ruhr. The last organized resistance in the Ruhr ended on April 18, with the capture of 317,000 German soldiers.

A growing concern for Eisenhower were rumors of a last-ditch stand deep in the mountains of southern Germany by remaining German forces. The Americans referred to this as the German "National Redoubt." Later events would show that Eisenhower's and the American Army's fear of a German National Redoubt proved to be completely unfounded.

With the Germans in the Ruhr ready to surrender, Eisenhower launched his three army groups eastward toward the Elbe and Mulde Rivers on April 11. The Mulde River runs into the Elbe at Dessau, Germany. On arriving at their objectives, Eisenhower's forces were to halt based on an agreement with Stalin to divide Germany in half. Patton's Third Army now consisted of 12 infantry and six armored divisions divided among four corps. Small patrols from the First Army made contact with the Soviet Army along the Elbe and Mulde Rivers on April 25. The first formal meetings between American and Russian divisional commanders took place the following day.

On April 14, Patton's Third Army approached within 10 miles of the western Czechoslovakia border and halted. Patton then received orders to regroup the Third Army in preparation for a new mission that would take it into Czechoslovakia and southward into Bavaria and Austria. The Austrian city of Linz fell to the Third Army on May 4. On May 7, the Germans signed surrender terms that were to become effective on May 9. May 8, however, became designated as V-E Day (Victory in Europe). In some remote areas fighting continued until May 11. During the period from April 22 to May 7, the Third Army took more than 200,000 German prisoners while suffering fewer than 2,400 casualties itself.

At the end of the war, the American Army compiled statistics on its casualties. In 281 days of combat, the Third Army lost 21,441 men killed, 99,224 wounded, and 16,200 missing. Nonbattle casualties were listed as 111,562. Patton's Third Army managed to seize 81,823 square miles of territory during its brief existence. Estimated casualties among the German forces that faced the Third Army in battle were 47,500 killed and 115,700 wounded. In total the Third Army captured 1,280,688 German military personnel between August 1, 1944, and May 13, 1945.

With the end of the war in Europe, Patton wanted to travel to the Pacific and fight the Japanese. His request was ignored, and he received the appointment of Military Governor of Bavaria. This job proved ill-suited to Patton's temperament. By the end of September 1945, Eisenhower relieved Patton from his job as military governor and took away his command of Third Army due to a number of statements he had made that Eisenhower deemed inappropriate. Patton then received command of the 15th Army, whose sole job was writing the history of the war in Europe. On December 9, 1945, on the way to a day of bird shooting in Germany, Patton was involved in a traffic accident in which he suffered serious injuries. He lived only 11 more days before passing away in his sleep on December 21. General George S. Patton, Jr., was buried with full military honors on December 24, 1945, at the American Military Cemetery in Hamm, just outside of Luxembourg.

BIBLIOGRAPHY

Blumenson, Martin. *Breakout and Pursuit.* United States Army in World War II. Washington, D.C.: U.S. Army, Office of the Chief of Military History, 1961.

Blumenson, Martin. *The Patton Papers,* 2 vols. Boston: Houghton Mifflin, 1974

Bradley, Omar N. *A Soldier's Story.* New York: Rand McNally, 1951; reprinted, New York: Rand McNally, 1978.

Cole, Hugh M. *The Ardennes: The Battle of the Bulge.* United States Army in World War II. Washington, D.C.: U.S. Army, Office of the Chief of Military History, 1965.

Cole, Hugh M. *The Lorraine Campaign.* United States Army in World War II. Washington, D.C.: U.S. Army, Office of the Chief of Military History, 1950.

D' Este, Carlo. *Patton: A Genius for War.* New York: Harper Collins Publishers, Inc., 1995.

Ellis, John. *The Sharp End: The Fighting Man in World War II.* New York: Charles Scribner's Sons, 1980.

Essame, H. *Patton: A Study in Command.* New York: Charles Scribner's Sons, 1974.

Forty, George. *U.S. Army Handbook.* Ian Allan Ltd., 1979.

Forty, George. *The Armies of George S. Patton.* London: Arms and Armour Press, 1996.

Greenfield, Kent R., Palmer, Robert R., and Wiley, Bell I. *The Organization of Ground Combat Troops.* United States Army in World War II. Washington, D.C.: U.S. Army, Office of the Chief of Military History, 1947.

Harrison, Gordon A. *Cross-Channel Attack.* United States Army in World War II. Washington, D.C.: U.S. Army, Office of the Chief of Military History, 1950.

Hastings, Max. *Overload: D-Day and the Battle for Normandy.* London: Pan Books Ltd., 1985.

Lee, Bruce. *Marching Orders: The Untold Story of World War II.* New York: Crown Publishers, Inc., 1995.

Irving, David. *The War Between the Generals: Inside the Allied High Command.* New York: Congdon & Lattes, Inc., 1981.

MacDonald, Charles B. *The Last Offensive.* United States Army in World War II. Washington, D.C.: U.S. Army, Office of the Chief of Military History, 1973.

MacDonald, Charles B. *The Siegfried Line Campaign.* United States Army in World War II. Washington, D.C.: U.S. Army, Office of the Chief of Military History, 1950.

Palmer, Robert R., Wiley, Bell I., and Keast, William R. *The Army Ground Forces: The Procurement and Training of Ground Combat Troops.* United States Army in World War II. Washington, D.C.: U.S. Army, Office of the Chief of Military History, 1948.

Patton, George S. Jr. *War as I Knew It.* Boston: Houghton Mifflin, 1947; reprint ed., New York: Bantam Books, 1981.

Pogue, Forest C. *The Supreme Command.* United States Army in World War II. Washington, D.C.: U.S. Army, Office of the Chief of Military History, 1954.

Province, Charles M. *The Unknown Patton.* New York: Hippocrence, 1983.

Province, Charles M. *Patton's Third Army.* New York: Hippocrence, 1991.

Province, Charles M. *Patton's One-Minute Messages.* Novato, Calif.: Presidio Press, 1995.

Weigley, Russell. *Eisenhower's Lieutenants.* Bloomington: Indiana University Press, 1981.

Whiting, Charles. *Patton.* New York: Ballantine Books, 1970.

Wilmot, Chester. *The Struggle for Europe.* New York: Carroll & Graf Publishers, Inc., 1986.

INDEX